SHADE & DANIEL
OLUKOYA

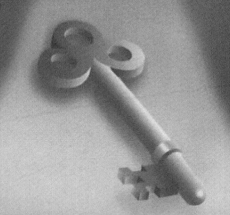

PRAYER
STRATEGIES
for
Singles

PRAYER STRATEGIES for SINGLES

Shade & Daniel Olukoya

PRAYER STRATEGIES FOR SINGLES

©1999 Dr. D. K. Olukoya

ISBN-13: 978-0692283721

Published - May, 1999
Reprinted - October, 2001
Reprinted - February, 2006
Reprinted - March, 2011

Published by:

The Battle Cry Christian Ministries

322, Herbert Macaulay Way, Yaba,

P. O. Box 12272, Ikeja, Lagos State, Nigeria.

Phone: 01 8044415, 0803-304-4239,

e-mail: sales@battlecryng.com

website: www.battlecryng.com

I salute my wonderful wife, Pastor Shade Olukoya for her invaluable support in the Ministry. I appreciate her unquantifiable support in the book Ministry as the cover designer, art editor and art adviser.

All the Scriptures are from the King James Version

Cover illustration by: Sister Shade Olukoya

Printed in Nigeria.

Other Publications by Dr. D. K. Olukoya, published and marketed by The Battle Cry Christian Ministries

1. 20 Marching Orders To Fulfill Your Destiny
2. 30 Things The Anointing Can Do For You
3. A-Z of Complete Deliverance
4. Abraham's Children In Bondage
5. Be Prepared
6. Bewitchment must die
7. Biblical Principles of Dream Interpretation
8. Born Great, But Tied Down
9. Breaking Bad Habits
10. Breakthrough Prayers For Business Professionals
11. Brokenness
12. Bringing Down The Power of God
13. Can God?
14. Can God Trust You?
15. Command The Morning
16. Consecration Commitment & Loyalty
17. Contending For The Kingdom
18. Connecting to The God of Breakthroughs
19. Criminals In The House Of God
20. Dancers At The Gate of Death
21. Dealing With Hidden Curses
22. Dealing With Local Satanic Technology
23. Dealing With Satanic Exchange
24. Dealing With The Evil Powers Of Your Father's House
25. Dealing With Tropical Demons
26. Dealing With Unprofitable Roots
27. Dealing With Witchcraft Barbers
28. Deliverance By Fire
29. Deliverance From Spirit Husband And Spirit Wife
30. Deliverance From The Limiting Powers

**Other Publications by Dr. D. K. Olukoya, published
and marketed by The Battle Cry Christian Ministries**

31. Deliverance of The Brain
32. Deliverance Of The Conscience
33. Deliverance Of The Head
34. Deliverance of The Tongue
35. Deliverance: God's Medicine Bottle
36. Destiny Clinic
37. Destroying Satanic Masks
38. Disgracing Soul Hunters
39. Divine Military Training
40. Divine Yellow Card
41. Dominion Prosperity
42. Drawers Of Power From The Heavenlies
43. Evil Appetite
44. Evil Umbrella
45. Facing Both Ways
46. Failure In The School Of Prayer
47. Fire For Life's Journey
48. For We Wrestle ...
49. Freedom Indeed
50. God's Key To A Happy Life
51. Holiness Unto The Lord
52. Holy Cry
53. Holy Fever
54. Hour Of Decision
55. How To Obtain Personal Deliverance
56. How To Pray When Surrounded By The Enemies
57. Idols Of The Heart
58. Is This What They Died For?
59. Killing The Serpent of Frustration
60. Let God Answer By Fire

**Other Publications by Dr. D. K. Olukoya, published
and marketed by The Battle Cry Christian Ministries**

61. Lord, Behold Their Threatening
62. Limiting God
63. Madness Of The Heart
64. Making Your Way Through The Traffic Jam of Life
65. Meat For Champions
66. Medicine For Winners
67. My Burden For The Church
68. Open Heavens Through Holy Disturbance
69. Overpowering Witchcraft
70. Paralysing The Riders And The Horse
71. Personal Spiritual Check-Up
72. Principles of Conclusive Prayers
73. Possessing The Tongue of Fire
74. Power Against Coffin Spirits
75. Power Against Destiny Quenchers
76. Power Against Dream Criminals
77. Power Against Local Wickedness
78. Power Against Marine Spirits
79. Power Against Spiritual Terrorists
80. Power To Recover Your Lost Glory
81. Power Must Change Hands
82. Pray Your Way To Breakthroughs
83. Prayer Is The Battle
84. Prayer Rain
85. Prayer Strategies For Spinsters And Bachelors
86. Prayer To Kill Enchantment
87. Prayer To Make You Fulfill Your Divine Destiny
88. Prayer Warfare Against 70 Mad Spirits
89. Prayers For Open Heavens
90. Prayers To Destroy Diseases And Infirmities

**Other Publications by Dr. D. K. Olukoya, published
and marketed by The Battle Cry Christian Ministries**

91. Prayers To Move From Minimum To Maximum
92. Praying Against The Spirit Of The Valley
93. Praying To Destroy Satanic Roadblocks
94. Praying To Dismantle Witchcraft
95. Principles Of Prayer
96. Release From Destructive Covenants
97. Revoking Evil Decrees
98. Safeguarding Your Home
99. Satanic Diversion Of The Black Race
100. Setting The Covens Ablaze
101. Seventy Sermons To Preach To Your Destiny
102. Silencing The Birds Of Darkness
103. Slaves Who Love Their Chains
104. Smite The Enemy And He Will Flee
105. Speaking Destruction Unto The Dark Rivers
106. Spiritual Education
107. Spiritual Growth And Maturity
108. Spiritual Warfare And The Home
109. Strategic Praying
110. Strategy Of Warfare Praying
111. Stop Them Before They Stop You
112. Students In The School Of Fear
113. Symptoms Of Witchcraft Attack
114. The Baptism of Fire
115. The Battle Against The Spirit Of Impossibility
116. The Dinning Table Of Darkness
117. The Enemy Has Done This
118. The Evil Cry Of Your Family Idol
119. The Fire Of Revival
120. The Great Deliverance

Other Publications by Dr. D. K. Olukoya, published and marketed by The Battle Cry Christian Ministries

121.   The Internal Stumbling Block
122.   The Lord Is A Man Of War
123.   The Mystery Of Mobile Curses
124.   The Mystery Of The Mobile Temple
125.   The Prayer Eagle
126.   The Power of Aggressive Prayer Warriors
127.   The Power of Priority
128.   The Pursuit Of Success
129.   The Seasons Of Life
130.   The Secrets Of Greatness
131.   The Serpentine Enemies
132.   The Skeleton In Your Grandfather's Cupboard
133.   The Slow Learners
134.   The Snake In The Power House
135.   The Spirit Of The Crab
136.   The star hunters
137.   The Star In Your Sky
138.   The Terrible Agenda
139.   The Tongue Trap
140.   The Unconquerable Power
141.   The Unlimited God
142.   The Vagabond Spirit
143.   The Way Of Divine Encounter
144.   The Wealth Transfer Agenda
145.   Tied Down In The Spirits
146.   Too Hot To Handle
147.   Turnaround Breakthrough
148.   Unprofitable Foundations
149.   Victory Over Satanic Dreams
150.   Victory Over Your Greatest Enemies

Other Publications by Dr. D. K. Olukoya, published and marketed by The Battle Cry Christian Ministries

151. Violent Prayers Against Stubborn Situations
152. War At The Edge Of Breakthroughs
153. Wasting The Wasters
154. Wasted At The Market Square of Life
155. Wealth Must Change Hands
156. What You Must Know About The House Fellowship
157. When God Is Silent
158. When the Battle is from Home .
159. When The Deliverer Need Deliverance
160. When Things Get Hard
161. When You Are Knocked Down
162. Where Is Your Faith
163. While Men Slept
164. Woman! Thou Art Loosed.
165. Your Battle And Your Strategy
166. Your Foundation And Destiny
167. Your Mouth And Your Deliverance

YORUBA PUBLICATIONS

1. ADURA AGBAYORI
2. ADURA TI NSI OKE NIDI
3. OJO ADURA

FRENCH PUBLICATIONS

1. PLUIE DE PRIERE
2. ESPIRIT DE VAGABONDAGE
3. EN FINIR AVEC LES FORCES MALEFIQUES DE LA MAISON DE TON PERE
4. QUE I'ENVOUTEMENT PERISSE
5. FRAPPEZ I'ADVERSAIRE ET IL FUIRA
6. COMMENT RECEVIOR LA DELIVRANCE DU MARI ET FEMME DE NUIT

Other Publications by Dr. D. K. Olukoya, published and marketed by The Battle Cry Christian Ministries

7. CPMMENT SE DELIVRER SOI-MEME
8. POVOIR CONTRE LES TERRORITES SPIRITUEL
9. PRIERE DE PERCEES POUR LES HOMMES D'AFFAIRES
10. PRIER JUSQU'A REMPORTER LA VICTOIRE
11. PRIERES VIOLENTES POUR HUMILIER LES PROBLEMES OPINIATRES
12. PRIERE POUR DETRUIRE LES MALADIES ET INFIRMITES
13. LE COMBAT SPIRITUEL ET LE FOYER
14. BILAN SPIRITUEL PERSONNEL
15. VICTOIRES SUR LES REVES SATANIQUES
16. PRIERES DE COMAT CONTRE 70 ESPIRITS DECHANINES
17. LA DEVIATION SATANIQUE DE LA RACE NOIRE
18. TON COMBAT ET TA STRATEGIE
19. VOTRE FONDEMENT ET VOTRE DESTIN
20. REVOQUER LES DECRETS MALEFIQUES
21. CANTIQUE DES CONTIQUES
22. LE MAUVAIS CRI DES IDOLES
23. QUAND LES CHOSES DEVIENNENT DIFFICILES
24. LES STRATEGIES DE PRIERES POUR LES CELIBATAIRES
25. SE LIBERER DES ALLIANCES MALEFIQUES
26. DEMANTELER LA SORCELLERIE
27. LA DELIVERANCE: LE FLACON DE MEDICAMENT DIEU
28. LA DELIVERANCE DE LA TETE
29. COMMANDER LE MATIN
30. NE GRAND MAIS LIE
31. POUVOIR CONTRE LES DEMOND TROPICAUX
32. LE PROGRAMME DE TRANFERT DE RICHESSE
33. LES ETUDIANTS A I'ECOLE DE LA PEUR
34. L'ETOILE DANS VOTRE CIEL
35. LES SAISONS DE LA VIE
36. FEMME TU ES LIBEREE

Other Publications by Dr. D. K. Olukoya, published and marketed by The Battle Cry Christian Ministries

ANNUAL 70 DAYS PRAYER AND FASTING PUBLICATIONS

1. Prayers That Bring Miracles
2. Let God Answer By Fire
3. Prayers To Mount With Wings As Eagles
4. Prayers That Bring Explosive Increase
5. Prayers For Open Heavens
6. Prayers To Make You Fulfill Your Divine Destiny
7. Prayers That Make God To Answer And Fight By Fire
8. Prayers That Bring Unchallengeable Victory And Breakthrough Rainfall Bombardments
9. Prayers That Bring Dominion Prosperity And Uncommon Success
10. Prayers That Bring Power And Overflowing Progress
11. Prayers That Bring Laughter And Enlargement Breakthroughs
12. Prayers That Bring Uncommon Favour And Breakthroughs
13. Prayers That Bring Unprecedented Greatness & Unmatchable Increase
14. Prayers That Bring Awesome Testimonies And Turn Around Breakthroughs
15. Prayers That Bring Glorious Restoration

ALSO OBTAINABLE AT

☞ **BATTLE CRY CHRISTIAN MINISTRIES**
Bookshop Shopping Mall, Prayer City
Km 12, Lagos / Ibadan Express way

☞ 2, Oregun Road, by Radio Bus Stop, Ikeja, Lagos
Km 12, Lagos / Ibadan Express way

☞ 54, Akeju Street, off Shipeolu Street, Palmgrove, Lagos

☞ Shop 26, Divine Grace Shopping Plaza, Isolo Jakande Estate, Isolo

☞ Christian bookstores.

TABLE OF CONTENTS

CHAPTER   . PAGE

1 HOW TO OBTAIN YOUR GOD-GIVEN PARTNER 12

2 POWER AGAINST MARRIAGE SCORPIONS   35

3 POWER AGAINST MARRIAGE SERPENTS   69

4 PRAYER SECTION

   Breaking Anti-Marriage Yoke   82

   Freedom From In-ordinate Affections
   and Soul Ties   96

   To Arrest Unprofitable Lateness
   In Marriage   98

   To Know God's Will in Marriage   102

   I Receive It   104

CHAPTER 1
HOW TO OBTAIN YOUR GOD-GIVEN PARTNER

MARRIAGE

Marriage, has become so bastardized in this modern age, that many people have given-up the idea of achieving an excellent marriage.

Homes are breaking up at an alarming rate. Divorce rate has reached an all-time high. More and more people are making up their mind never to get married, simply because they believe that marriage no longer works.

A lot of people have been married times without number. Others have decided to give birth to children without accepting the responsibility of marriage. Some even decide to live with a man or a woman of their choice as long as the relationship works.

Funny enough, some people have tried to banish marriage from their thoughts. If we look at the mess which marriage has become, we are likely to conclude that the situation is awfully bad. However, all right thinking people know that it is not wise to look at marriage the way man has made it. Rather, we should look at marriage the way God made it.

Marriage is God's idea. God had a beautiful idea when He created the marriage institution. It is a divinely ordained institution. Just like everything which God made, marriage was designed to be a glorious and blissful experience. In God's programme, marriage is the best thing that can ever happen to man. It embodies the epitome of God's desire for His Children.

It is God's intention to grant His people a foretaste of what to expect in heaven through the institution of marriage.

A happy home is a little heaven on earth. It is the demonstration of the possibilities of faith and grace.

Through marriage, the highest ideals of the Christian faith are relished and cherished by all. Apart from salvation, it is the greatest grace which man can enjoy.

A home that is established by God is greater and higher than anything which man has ever attempted to create or establish.

Marriage is the beginning and the end of life. It is the center of human existence and the school of experience.

God is the architect, the planner and the builder of marriage. The Bible says marriage is honourable. When two people who love and honour the Lord are brought together in holy matrimony with a decision to make God the central focus of their lives, such people will surely experience, enjoy and attain an excellent marriage. In the words of the scripture, they will enjoy and experience what eyes have never seen, ears have never heard and what has never entered the heart of man. Their experience can only be described in superlative language.

Beloved, I have tried to describe God's perfect will for

your marriage but I am not going to pretend that all is well with every Christian marriage today.

THE DEVIL'S ATTACK ON MARRIAGES

The devil has attacked the institution of marriage more than any other thing on earth. He, as it were, has taken his headquarters to the home. He has mustered all his forces against the home. He has an array of various groups of soldiers against Christian as well as non-Christian homes.

What you may be going through now may not be God's perfect will for you. But the fact that the home has been attacked shows us the importance which God as well as Satan have placed on it.

Some people ask me, "G. O., why is my home attacked?" The reasons are not far-fetched. The devil is attacking your marriage because he knows that if that area of your life is settled then the battle would be easy for you. That is why, he has concentrated his energy towards giving you more problems in that area than you can cope with. He knows the prospects that lie ahead for you. That is why, he is standing by and fighting relentlessly against you in that area.

The battles you have experienced so far should not make you give up. Rather, you should turn them to challenges. You must always remember that Satan always attack what is good.

14

AVOID GREAT MISTAKE

A lot of people today have made great mistakes in the area of marriage. Some of these people have got to the point of no return. They can no longer amend what has gone wrong. However, all those who are yet to take the all important journey into marriage are very fortunate. They have the opportunity of looking before taking a plunge into marriage.

Bachelors and spinsters are very fortunate. They have the opportunity of examining all the cards that are laid on the table, before taking this important step that will determine their success or failure in life.

A good marriage, will expose you to a sort of heaven on earth while a bad one will expose you to hell on earth.

The most important factor in achieving a successful marriage is the choice you make. If you make a good choice, then you are sure that you have started on the right note. But a bad choice leaves you with a faulty foundation which will work against your marriage sooner or later.

A lot of people who are married today have discovered that the great mistakes of their lives can be traced to the choice which they made. Therefore, you must put a lot of factors into consideration if you want to enjoy your marriage.

Most of the married people around us today are still staying together because they are ashamed of the consequences of separation. They know of course, that the marriage has collapsed completely. They are only staying together because they do not want anyone to feel that all the money, time and effort which went into the marriage are wasted. They are probably afraid of what neighbours and friends would say. That is why they are still staying under the same roof.

To make a mistake in marriage is worse than living in hell. Unfortunately, many are in this situation.

A brother felt that he had prayed and took a sister to his pastor as his choice in marriage. The pastor asked to know whether the brother was really sure of what he was saying. He answered in the affirmative, and then got married after a few months. One month later, the brother ran back to the pastor saying, "Pastor, please can you grant me a divorce? I am tired of the woman whom you gave to me in marriage." The pastor said, "I can't understand what you are saying, divorce? That's impossible. Don't you know that once you are married, you are married forever? There is nothing like divorce and re-marriage. If you divorce your wife, you are playing with hell fire."

The brother said, "Oh is that a problem? Going to hell fire? That's not a problem. I am already living in hell in my home. I don't think there is any hell greater than what I am passing through. The woman, who I am married to is worse than the devil. I prefer to divorce her and go to hell. I prefer to live with the devil instead of living with that woman. Allow me to get rid of the hell which my home has become. I think I would be able to cope with hell fire later," the man said.

The pastor made him to know that the decision to marry that woman was actually his own and that he should be ready to face the consequences of the decision which he took. That is what it means to face the consequences of one's decision.

Another brother got into an embarrassing situation when he made up his mind to marry a particular lady. What actually happened was that the lady in question came to him for counselling and prayer but the young man became fascinated and began to think of marrying her. He took the lady to the pastor to announce his intention to marry her. The young man did not discover anything while the courtship lasted. He only observed that the lady was fond of keeping her head-scarf on, all the time. He was even happy about it, thinking that the lady must be a very serious and prayerful Christian.

Their marriage plan went on without any hitch. The marriage ceremony was elaborate. The man left the church thinking that he had married a wonderful lady. When they got home, he decided to lay his hands on the head of the wife, being a member of the prayer warrior. By the time he placed his hands on her head, alas, there were two horns. When he opened his eyes, blood was dripping from his hands. The two horns had wounded him. He became confused and did not know what to do.

Here is a man who had just married a new wife. Yet, the step which he had taken became a problem rather than a pleasant experience. He continued to live with his newly wedded wife for days, weeks and months without being able to move close to her. He was always haunted by the fact that he had married a strange human being. He contemplated divorce, but knew that it was virtually impossible to think of divorcing her and taking up a new wife. He had made a choice and there was no going back. Even when he complained to his pastor, he was simply told to take it as a battle, moreover that he happened to be a member of the prayer warrior team.

People should prayerfully take their time to make a choice which they will never live to regret.

A sister also had an experience which is quite close to the one I have just narrated. When those who are not married read certain stories, they sometimes wonder whether such things can happen. But I want you to know that a lot of people go through strange experiences which they cannot disclose to anybody. Those who go through these horrible and strange experiences know that what they are passing through is real.

The sister, whose story I am narrating now, was serious and God-fearing. Instead of praying and carefully selecting her future husband, she decided to pick on just anybody because she felt that she had waited for too long. As soon as she found someone who appeared presentable, she rushed to the pastor to announce her intention to marry the man. The pastor did not want her to make a mistake so he asked her if she was sure that the step she was taking had been approved and sanctioned by God. "Yes", she said. "I am sure of the step I am taking, I have lots of testimonies to back up my claim. I would not have come to present the man to you if I did not do my home-work thoroughly. He is God's will for me." She concluded.

The pastor said, "Well if you are sure that you have taken the right step, you can go ahead and marry him but I want you to remember that there is no going back once you get married. The moment you are married, you are married for life. There is no divorce and remarriage." That was how the sister decided to go ahead with the man and the marriage was conducted. She married the man and left the church with high hopes.

However, her expectations were never fulfilled. In fact, the marriage ended up becoming a nightmare. She was shocked, and almost fainted when right before her, the man she married in the church suddenly transformed into a gorilla. She felt as if the ground should open up and swallow her. That was how her gorilla husband bounced on her and gave her marks all over her body. She could not recover from the shock for a very long time. To talk about her plight was impossible as no one would easily believe her story.

The man continued to turn into a gorilla and gave her nasty marks on her body each time they were alone. To walk out of the marriage was impossible. After all, she said that she was very sure of the decision she made. That is why it never pays to be in a hurry. Who knows, you can pick somebody like that if you decide to marry whoever you come across. You must not toy with the choice you make in the area of marriage.

THOROUGH PREPARATION

The second thing you must take note of as you prepare to get married, is that thorough preparation is necessary for a happy marriage. You must prepare adequately if you want to experience a lasting marriage relationship. You must read your Bible and find out the areas in which you have to make preparations.

I want you to learn a lesson from God. He never does anything without proper preparation. He is a God of preparation. You should also learn a lesson from the ministry of the Lord Jesus. He does not do anything without preparing for it. Wherever He would go to minister, He would send some of His disciples ahead of Him to prepare the way.

Noah also prepared when the flood was about to come upon the earth. He spent one hundred and twenty years in preparation.

John the Baptist was the forerunner of Jesus Christ. His mission was to prepare the hearts of people for the coming of the Lord Jesus Christ.

From these examples, we discover that preparation is needed, for any important thing to succeed.

The more preparation you make, the greater your chances of succeeding in marriage. You can buy a car within five minutes. You can also acquire a great property within a short time. You can take business decisions without batting an eyelid. You must know that you can not compare anything with an important decision like getting married or building a home.

Those who have attempted to rush into marriage, have only discovered that although, it is easy to rush into it, it is not so easy to jump out of it.

The foundation of marriage must be well laid for the building on it to be solid.

Marriage is not what you can jump into, through love at first sight. The Bible does not recognise such a hasty decision. You must also prepare if you want your marriage to be what God intended it to be. Jesus said, "In my father's house there are many mansions. I go to prepare a place for you." That statement underscores the importance of preparation before any important project is handled.

Therefore, personal preparation cannot be over emphasised. You have to make preparations in the following areas: laying the foundation for your future life, ministry, prayer, development of Christian character, learning how to cope with serious life situations, and so on.

• Relationship with God

However, the most important preparation which you need to make is in the area of your relationship with God. If you want God to be involved in your marriage, you must start a vibrant relationship with Him. Anyone who is not born again will discover sooner or later that the practical nitty-gritty of marriage cannot be handled without experiencing and receiving the power to become a child of God.

- **Maturity**

Another preparation which you ought to make is in the area of maturity.

You must be mature physically, emotionally, and psychologically. The Bible did not say, "Therefore, shall a boy or a girl leave his father and mother and be joined to his wife/husband." Marriage is for mature men and women. Boys and girls are not ready for marriage.

You must be mature materially. You must have a job, a business or a trade. A man who is still sleeping on a mat in his father's living room is not ready for marriage. A lady who has nothing doing is not prepared for marriage. Both partners must have a good source of income that will sustain the marriage and cope with the financial responsibilities involved in marriage.

You must also be spiritually mature before going into marriage. You must get yourself to a spiritual level where, at least, you will be able to pray and know whether God is saying Yes or No. The issue of marriage is so important that if it makes you a prayer warrior, it is alright. When you listen to the stories of other people, you will discover that no price can be too costly to pay in the area of prayer.

Some years ago, a man grabbed his wife, gave her a

22

razor blade and asked her to cut herself to get some blood from her body. Initially, the woman was reluctant saying, "Why must I do so?" The husband shouted at her, "you better do it now or else I will kill you". The woman quickly went ahead to make incisions on her body, not knowing what next to expect. The man took the blade from her hand and cut himself. He ran to the kitchen and brought a cup with which he collected some blood from her body as well as from his. He diluted the blood with wine and demanded that both of them should drink the concoction.

The woman was so afraid that she had to close her eyes to drink the mixture of blood and wine. The man also took a sip. He turned to her and said: "With this blood covenant, you are no longer free to have anything to do with any other man throughout your life. If you do so , it is instant death." Unfortunately, the man died in a ghastly motor accident. The woman was not able to marry again because she had formed a powerful blood covenant with her late husband. She lived the rest of her life in misery and woe. She became a prisoner of a powerful blood covenant.

I pity ladies who enter into covenant with men who are not even committed to them in marriage. People also go into covenant by saying, "I love you, I will never leave you. If I leave you, let terrible things happen to me." Such statements are hidden covenants. If you breach them, you will reap the consequences.

- **Clear goals and pure motives**
  Another area of preparation which you will do well to

look into, is in the area of clear goals and pure motive. Do not go into a relationship with a selfish motive. If your motive is selfish, God will not back you up. Don't go into a relationship because you want to be loved. Your motive must be clear, pure and godly. You must also desire a person whose life and character will enhance your spiritual growth. If you go for someone whom you have to teach the elementary principles of the scriptures, that person may end up pulling you down.

I remember the story of a sister who wanted to marry someone whose spiritual life was below expectation. I told her that I would like to see her prospective husband. At least I wanted to pray with both of them. When the sister invited the man, the man became furious and refused to come. He told the sister, "I don't understand what you are saying. I don't have any business with any pastor. All I want is to get married to you." The sister tried her best to persuade the man but he refused. The sister narrated her experience to me and I started to wonder why the man bluntly refused to come and see me.

I asked the sister, "Are you sure that this man is a child of God. Why is he against prayer?" The sister said, "I believe that he is born again. He actually told me that he has been a Christian for twelve years." I told her that I would still go ahead to pray and check things up with the Lord. When I prayed, I was baffled by what I saw. I saw a very tall sister dragging a baby in three piece suit to the altar. Then, it

24

dawned on me that they were going to have problems with their marriage. I told her what I saw. But she assured me that she was sure of what she was doing and that she has prayed about the man.

They eventually got married and the sister discovered that she had walked into a dangerous relationship. As soon as they settled down to enjoy the new marriage, the man began to behave in a funny manner. He started by shouting at her. Then he began to give her occasional slaps. Before she knew what was happening, he began to threaten her with a gun. That was how the woman continued to live in fear day in, day out. Things became so bad one day, that a Christian brother had to rush in to their house to prevent the man from shooting the sister. The man actually fired the gun, but it narrowly missed the ear of the brother who went to separate them.

The peace maker brother ran to me gasping for breath. He said, "Is that how people die? G. O., I almost lost my life today. I went to the house of brother and sister so and so. The husband fired a shot which almost blew up my head. I have never seen that kind of a thing before." Later, the wife ran to me to narrate her ordeal. That was how it became clear to her that she had actually taken the wrong step. She had no option but to carry a cross which God never meant for her. I had to give her some prayer points and anointing oil so that she can experience some measure of peace in her home. I warned her but she thought she knew what she was doing. Her decision to marry somebody who was of a lower spiritual status bounced back on her.

Prayer Strategies for Singles

• Prayer

Another area that needs proper preparation, is prayer. Marriage is a life long issue. It requires the best prayer effort that can be given to it. You must take the time to handle every area of your marital life with prayer. You must pray about your choice, your spouse, your future, home, children, relationship with your spouse and your common goals.

• Hospitality

One of the things that ensures success in marriage is hospitality. If you are not hospitable, caring and friendly, you are not ready for marriage. A man or woman who is unfriendly, quarrelsome and selfish, cannot make a good husband or wife. Those who decide to have nothing to do with others as well as those who say that they have no time for other people are not prepared for marriage. If you excuse your short comings by calling yourself an introvert, you are merely deceiving yourself. You are only covering up the deficiencies in your character.

• Don't Be In A Hurry

An African proverb says: "Never be in a hurry to lick a hot soup." If you do so, it will scorch your tongue and you may never enjoy the soup. "Slow and steady", they say "wins the race." Those who are in a hurry, generally make serious mistakes. The Bible says, "He that believeth shall not make haste." If you build your house in a hurry, you must be ready to face the consequences should it collapse on your head. You must not be in a hurry in situations that are of eternal consequence.

After taking care of the preliminary preparations necessary for a successful marriage, you must go ahead to consider the prayer strategy that must be put in place to obtain your God-given partner. The moment you are ready to pray, you will receive the person whom God made for you as your partner. You must know the prayer steps to take.

How do you pray this kind of prayer? The kind of prayer I am referring to is different from the regular prayer you pray in other areas of life. Praying to know God's will in marriage differs significantly from the prayer of deliverance. This kind of prayer can be likened to a diving magnet which is used to fish out your own particular spouse.

It is not proper to lump this prayer with other general prayers in life. To take this prayer only when you have finished general prayers is to demonstrate your lack of seriousness concerning the issue of marriage. To make the prayer of the choice of your partner in marriage as a mere appendage during your regular quiet time is to give the impression that it is an insignificant item. That kind of attitude will make you an easy prey for the devil.

Some people hold night vigils because of the problems in other areas of their lives but do not think of giving the issue of marriage much attention. Unknown to such people, they are neglecting a weighty matter that has eternal consequences. Do you know that apart from your spiritual life, the next most important thing is your marriage.

You need to pray aggressively concerning your marriage because a lot of forces are fighting against marriage. A lot of people have discovered that some powers have been giving them serious problems in the area of marriage. Each time such people make up their mind to marry, something suddenly comes upon them and makes them to be completely disenchanted about the whole issue. One moment, they are excited about getting married to a particular person, the next moment, they find themselves hating the person. Then the relationship is dissolved. Another one is started only for the same problem to reoccur again.

That kind of situation continues time and again until the person decides to give up the thought of ever getting married again. That kind of situation can only be handled through aggressive prayer. In fact, it takes deliverance prayers to handle such a tough case.

HOW TO PRAY IN KNOWING GOD'S WILL IN MARRIAGE

What then are the general steps to be taken, in order to pray to know God's will in marriage?

• Allocate a specific time to it

You must not handle this kind of prayer hapharzardly. You must be definite about it. For example, if you can choose a particular day of the week when you devote an ample time to pray about the issue of marriage, you will achieve wonderful results. Such an allocated time must be regular. Marriage is so important that apportioning one day to it is a wise investment. From that particular day, you will focus on the issue of marriage and give less thought to other areas of life.

That reminds me of what somebody said: "What is good needs prayer so that it does not become bad. What is bad needs prayer so that it does not become worse. What is barely okay needs prayer so that it can be taken to the maximum level." You must therefore, withdraw your prayer concerning marriage from the general list.

● **Relax and focus your attention on God**

This kind of prayer cannot be handled with a divided heart. The prayer that will magnetize your correct partner to you cannot be handled with levity. You cannot handle it with a divided mind or with a heart that is filled with anxiety and doubt. It is not a prayer to be prayed only when somebody else's marriage is announced. To handle that kind of prayer when you are sad, discouraged and tensed up is to start on a wrong note. To shed some kind of crocodile tears while handling this issue is to be involved with some kind of satanic entertainment.

The Bible says, "Be still and know that I am God." If you pray while your heart is not settled, you will make mistakes. When you are burdened, discouraged, sad, despondent and faithless, you will not pray effectively. You must take certain steps, to overcome the initial hindrances.

You must recognize the fact that God wants you to be still before Him. Let me give you some hints on what you can do, to maintain a proper focus when handling the issue of marriage in prayer.

• *Praise and worship*

Praise and worship ushers you into the presence of God and makes you to focus.

• *Meditate upon the word of God*

The word of God shifts your attention away from worry and anxiety and places your heart on the promises of God.

• *Meditate on God's sufficiency and greatness*

Look away from your mountain and concentrate on God's mightiness.

• *Submit your mind to God*

It takes a lot of discipline, to submit one's mind unto God. Once you are able to cultivate the habit of keeping your mind focused on God, it becomes part of you. If you make use of these four methods, you will be able to pray without distraction. You must therefore give adequate time to speak to God.

• *Confess any sin which the Holy Spirit is convicting you of and receive God's forgiveness*

Do not sweep anything under the carpet. Seek the

assistance of the Holy Spirit for whatever you know you have done wrong. You must also go ahead to forgive everyone who has offended you, no matter how painful the offences were. Jesus said: "Forgive us our trespasses as we forgive all those who trespass against us."

You cannot handle this kind of prayer successfully while you are still holding grudges against those who have offended you. But when you confess your sins, receive forgiveness from God and go ahead to forgive all those who have offended you then, you have a pure heart before God and you are ready to receive from Him. If you neglect this third factor, you may not be able to receive answer from God.

The devil knows that, if you scale through the area of marriage, you are going to become a thorn in his flesh and will not allow him any rest. So, he will look for ways of hindering you. Once there is a legal reason, satan will petition God by pointing at facts like unconfessed sins and lack of forgiveness in your life. If the petition is based on legal reasons, it may work against you.

- **Pray for the Holy Spirit to fill you and overflow**

It is easier for a man or a woman who is filled with the Holy Spirit to receive a clear information or direction from God. If you have not yet received the baptism of the Holy Spirit, you must pray for the experience. Don't go into

31

marriage without being filled with the Holy Ghost. You may be looking for a serious trouble as there are many tough areas of marriage which someone who is not Spirit-filled cannot handle.

The Bible says: "For we know not what to pray for. The Spirit himself helpeth our infirmities with groanings that cannot be uttered" (Rom.8:26).

This passage shows us that the human mind is not capable of knowing how to approach prayer perfectly. When you are Spirit-filled, you find it easy to pray correctly. For example, you can pray in tongues concerning your marriage.

- **Cover yourself with the blood of Jesus and proclaim the Lordship of the Lord over your life**
When you begin to pray about marriage, you are getting into a very important area which the devil will try very hard to fight against. You cannot pray about marriage without attracting hostility from the camp of the devil. That is why, you have to cover yourself with the blood of Jesus.

- **Expect God to speak to you**
You must be expectant. That places the responsibility of waiting, upon you. The Bible says, "My soul, wait thou only upon God. For my expectation is from him." (Psalm 62:5). This kind of prayer cannot be approached with the "hit and run" method. You may not hear anything for

a week or a month, you must wait all the same. Don't be discouraged. You cannot pressurize God or coerce Him to dance to your tune. He will speak to you in His own way and at His own time.

However, you must remember that there are three types of voice: the voice of God, the voice of the devil and your own voice. But the moment you have covered yourself with the blood of Jesus and proclaimed the lordship of Jesus upon your life, the devil will not be able to speak to you.

● **Be determined**

Stick to your prayers, no matter the problem that may arise. You must refuse to give up. Do not rest, until you know that you have received your desired breakthrough. Make sure that you actually get to a point when you have not only got answers but when you have also secured an overwhelming peace.

In other words, pray until the peace of God settles in your life. If that peace does not settle in your heart you have to continue praying. Don't allow anything to discourage you. You may see conflicting visions. There are days when prayer will look like a difficult task. Continue to pray, all the same. Remember that prayer is hard work. Nobody has a natural likeness for prayer. Be persistent. Your miracle may be around the corner. Be determined. Refuse to give up at the edge of your miracle.

● **Deliberately refuse to worry**

You cannot get any result by worrying. Worry and anxiety negate faith and show lack of confidence in God.

Prayer Strategies for Singles

• Support your prayer with fasting

Fasting energises prayer. It makes your spirit sharper. If you are able to fulfil these conditions, then, you are ready to take the prayer points. The prayer points which are written below have produced wonderful results. Many people who were bachelors and spinsters before used these prayer points and they are married today. If you can take the prayer points with all seriousness, you will experience the same result.

PRAYER POINTS

1. O Lord, let Your perfect will be fulfilled in my life, in the name of Jesus.
2. O Lord, magnetize my divinely ordained partner to me and keep all the others away in the name of Jesus.
3. I refuse to cooperate with any anti-marriage curse and covenant, in the name of Jesus.
4. I cancel, every bewitchment, fashioned against my settling down in marriage, in the name of Jesus.
5. I cancel, every spiritual wedding, conducted consciously or unconsciously on my behalf, in the name of Jesus.

CHAPTER TWO
POWER AGAINST MARRIAGE SCORPIONS

FORCES TO BATTLE

Man, has a lot of forces to contend with. These forces are more in number and more wicked when it comes to the area of marriage. These hostile forces come in various shapes and forms and attack every department of marriage and the family. The odds and the hurdles which have to be scaled are just too many. There is no denying the fact that, the devil is a specialist in stopping every good thing at the stage of infancy. That is why, he always arrange lots of hindrances and stumbling blocks against every genuine effort. You therefore, must be ready to deal with these forces.

You need to ensure, that you have enough power to combat the forces which the devil arranges against the success of your journey into marriage. You should never allow the devil, to intimidate you. You must get to a point in your spiritual life, when you no longer fear any form of attack from the devil. You must always live in consciousness of the fact that the one who lives in you is greater than the one who lives in the world. When you become conscious of the fact that you are more than conquerors through the Lord Jesus Christ, you will be conscious of victory whenever you face any battle.

SERPENTS AND SCORPIONS

The Bible says, "Behold I give unto you power to tread on serpents and scorpions and over all the power of the enemy and nothing shall by any means hurt you" (Luke 10:19). This popular passage centers on the authority of the believer. Two words stand out from the verse: "serpents and scorpions."

• What they represent

What do serpents and scorpions represent? They represent the powers of darkness in all their ramifications. It is common knowledge that, these two creatures are extremely dangerous. Nevertheless, we are commanded and mandated to tread upon them.

No doubt, God knows that they are loaded with terrible venoms and poisonous stings, yet He commanded us to tread upon them. Doesn't that sound like achieving the impossible? Not at all. God has made a wonderful provision for us to be able to achieve what He has commanded us to do. That is why the Bible says, "Thy shoes shall be as iron" (Deut 33:25). You can step on anything if your shoes are made of iron. You will live without fear. You will be able to trample upon anything.

If a snake tries to bite an iron shoe, the snake is looking for trouble. A scorpion which tries to sting a shoe made of iron is just wasting its time. The moment God gives you iron shoes you become unbeatable.

The presence of snakes and scorpions in the world gives

us an awareness of the fact that there are countless number of enemies in the world. Snakes and scorpions are dangerous creatures. If you have seen a snake in action, you would have noticed that it is difficult to predict its movement. You really cannot know what it is thinking about because it will be expressionless. Do you know that, that is exactly how some enemies behave? You cannot tell whether they are happy with you or not. They are always indifferent. Ask anybody who has ever been bitten by a snake and they would tell you that they did not know that the snake was aiming at them.

There is no one, who does not want to experience success and breakthrough in life. In fact, God has not designed anyone to fail. Problems and failures are satanic products. The devil is behind all kinds of hindrances, evil attacks, failures, sicknesses and everything that has ever constituted problems to men and women.

Something happened recently when I was invited to minister in a particular church which shows that the devil would do everything possible to make men and women lose good opportunities in life. The topic I handled in that service was "Soul Traders." We had not started praying when somebody screamed from the back saying, "Oh they have come. They want to kill me." The ushers managed to carry him out of the service before the service went on.

Five minutes later, another man screamed saying, "They have come here to kill me because they know that I am going to become the president of Nigeria." Those who were around the man quickly carried their Bibles and looked for other seats. I continued. The third person screamed again and he was also carried out of the meeting.

Do you know why those things were happening? The devil knew that his days were numbered, in the lives of those who attended that programme. He did not want to loose his hold over the three people who were carried out. That was why he attacked them right in the meeting. He knew that if those people had remained under my ministration, that day would have ended all their problems. That was why he created problems which hindered them from benefitting from a life-time opportunity, to get their problems solved once and for all. The devil knew that they were going to get out of his cage. That was why he engineered various problems which hindered them.

We are fighting against very intelligent enemies. That is why Jesus called them serpents and scorpions. Jesus commands us to be as wise as serpents.

WHAT THEN IS THE WISDOM OF THE SERPENT?

The wisdom is the ability to bite someone and disappear. The serpent is so clever that it can hide under leaves and grasses without being detected by its victim. It can also move towards its victim without being noticed or detected.

The scorpion is equally crafty. It is also expressionless. A scorpion appears harmless on the surface. It hides its poison around its tail. It walks past its victim harmlessly, only to stretch forth its tail and sting wickedly.

Why are these serpents and scorpions, bent on stopping people by all means?

It is simply because they know that if these wicked creatures are exposed, the people will end up killing the scorpions and serpents. These scorpions and serpents are spirits, with unusual powers and intelligence. Their goal is to bite, sting, and destroy. These creatures have no respect for race, nation, person or status.

Serpents and scorpions abound everywhere. The evil powers, do not want the truth concerning them, exposed. And they are terrible liars. They vary in their power and wickedness. However, I need to emphasize the fact that they are highly organized. They have been specifically established and instructed to fight against marriages.

I have seen lots of people in African nations, who got into trouble when they were babies. A man became a member of the church three years ago. He came with bundles of problems. He is now above 60 years old. His problem started on the very day he was born. It is customary for parents to consult soothsayers in order to receive divination concerning the future of their children. His parents were illiterates.

When the local soothsayer was consulted, he gave the parents the result of his findings. "The baby you have brought to me today has a unique star. In fact, I have never seen anyone with such a fantastic future. I saw him sitting on the throne surrounded by white men and women who were bowing down before him. He is going to be a king, a sort of great man among white men and women. So you must take care of him. This is the child who is going to put an end to all your problems."

The parents were not at home with the strange divination. They asked the fetish priest, "Do you mean that he is going to travel abroad and leave us alone in the village. Who, then, would take care of us, we shall suffer, becoming a king among white men and women does not mean a thing to us."

Then they went ahead to tell the soothsayer to do whatever he can to change the future of the child. The fetish priest accepted to do what they wanted. However, he told them that they must be ready to bring the baby's umbilical cord to his shrine. The parents rushed back and brought it. Then the fetish priest tied a very heavy stone to it, entered a boat and went right to the middle of a big river and threw the umbilical cord there. He then assured the parents that as long as the umbilical cord was under the sea, the man will never travel anywhere beyond his country. That was how the parents and the fetish priest tampered with the destiny of the brother.

You need to have an encounter with the brother in question, to appreciate the level of his suffering in life. He is so intelligent, that if he found his way outside the shores of his country, he would have become a world class genius. The brother is so intelligent and gifted, that if you appoint him as secretary to any meeting and the meeting lasted for three hours, he can listen and reproduce every discussion without writing anything down. The report which he will give you, will make you think that he had a tape recorder hidden somewhere.

He is so intelligent, that one wonders why he was not able to achieve anything. The man was supposed to shine among whites but his destiny was turned upside down. Through his umbilical cord, he became chained to his country. The man spent more than fifty years without discovering himself. The Lord opened his eyes and revealed the secret of his life to him when he came in contact with me. It was then he discovered that he had been diverted to a wrong place when he was one day old. The unfortunate thing was that he had lost almost every opportunity before he came across this ministry.

The powers of the scorpion and serpent have only one duty: to hinder people, from getting to where God wants them to be. They would either give people a bad marriage or prevent them from getting married at all. The purpose of doing this, is to keep their victims preoccupied with problems so that they are never able to destroy the serpents and the scorpions.

The forces behind serpents and scorpions are against your salvation. The only other most important thing in life is marriage.

Do you even know that, the institution of marriage came up before the institution of the church? In other words, God started marriage before He started the church.

41

Prayer Strategies for Singles

The devil knows that God is highly interested in marriage, that is why he is fighting tirelessly against it. Discouragement cannot solve any problem. Crying or shedding tears, cannot give solution to your problem in the area of marriage. The devil does not recognize tears.

Christians today should discard the anointing of Jeremiah, the weeping prophet, and ask for the anointing of Jesus, the One who has authority and power over all circumstances. This becomes necessary because, the devil has increased the tempo of his battle against marriage. Those who are timid, weak-minded and fearful cannot defeat the devil. What you need therefore, is not discouragement or shedding of tears. The Bible says "The righteous shall be as bold as a lion."

Discouragement is the most effective tool in the hand of the devil. No matter how many hours, days, weeks and months you have spent in prayer, one day of depression and discouragement, can cancel everything you have laboured for. One day of depression can cancel all your previous faith, fasting, confession and prayer efforts. This is why, many people have not been able to achieve anything tangible in the area of marriage. They take one step forward and four steps backward whenever discouragement comes.

A sister came to complain to me that she has prayed without getting any result.

She said:" I have come to tell you that I am fed up. I am no longer ready to wait for God's direction. I am already thirty two years old. Those who were coming to me for marriage over the years are Alhajis and irresponsible men. I am fed up. I have served Jesus for six years and He has disappointed me. I cannot lay hold on anything as what I have received from God all these years. I have now decided to do it my own way. Don't be surprised, if you suddenly find me pregnant any moment from now. I wouldn't mind becoming a third or a fourth wife. I am sad, because people are laughing at me. All my younger sisters have got married, and they are all asking me to pack out of the family house. I am no longer ready to keep on hoping, that God will one day direct me. I have come to inform you that, I have finally made up my mind, that I will just go ahead and get pregnant for just any man."

I looked at her and shook my head. I was extremely sad. Do you know what made me sad? As the lady was standing before me I saw an angel right beside her carrying her wedding gown. God had not forgotten her. The angel was only waiting for God to finish dealing with the sister's enemies before handing the wedding gown to her. What she did not know was that if the wedding gown had been given to her when her enemies were very much around they would have snatched it from her.

God is never late. Delay is not denial. Perhaps the little delay you are experiencing, is necessary for God to thoroughly deal with every serpent and scorpion who are likely to constitute problems to your marriage. That is why, those who avoid waiting and decide to rush into marriage often experience mysterious problems.

Prayer Strategies for Singles

We have cases of people who got married and died either on their on the wedding day or during child birth. They would have escaped such calamities, if they had taken the time to deal with serpents and scorpions. They would also have enjoyed their marriages, if they have allowed God to deal all the necessary blows on all the enemies of their marriages.

Therefore, don't be in a hurry, you must give God time, to sort out all the enemies.

You must be ready to strike a balance between faith and warfare. Nobody should be deceived by simplistic statement made by modern-day fake preachers. You must not allow anyone to deceive you by telling you that the devil is dead. The devil is not dead. He is alive and active.

Some preachers give people the impression that the devil has no power. Where then did the magicians who challenged Moses got the power to turn their rods to serpents? Certainly, they did not use the power of the Holy Spirit.

When you tell some people, to face the battles of their lives, they would tell you that Jesus has won the battle and that they do not need to fight any battle again. Others would tell you, " I don't care about any battle because the devil is under my feet." Such statements are half-truths. Nobody contests the finished work of Christ, but you have to enforce what Jesus had finished or settled. You must fight to possess your possession.

Prayer Strategies for Singles

You can call the devil any name. But never call him a fool, because he is very intelligent. He has dealt with men and women for more than six thousand years. He is much more intelligent than human beings. He was in heaven before and he was able to acquire a lot of wisdom through his staying in the presence of God before he fell. He knew how God organizes the various departments in heaven. He had therefore stolen from the wisdom behind the spiritual and physical structures in heaven. He now uses that wisdom in his own kingdom.

Therefore, the devil knows what to fight against. He has continued to focus his warfare, on hindering the right matches or preventing the right people from discovering and accepting themselves.

Secondly, he hinders many people from getting married at all.

Thirdly, he causes late marriages.

Fourthly, he causes problems, between those who are planning to get married.

The devil is sufficiently aware of the fact that, there is no force on earth, that can hinder a couple that is completely united with each other.

More than anything else, the devil dreads the prayer of a husband and wife whose hearts agree as touching any one thing in prayer. That is why, the devil's priority, is to attack the foundation of any marriage. The devil knows that you are going to become dangerous to his kingdom if he should allow you to get married without any problem. That is why the Bible has said, "If the foundation be destroyed, what can the righteous do?" You must not allow the devil to tamper with your foundation.

I remember the interesting story of a brother, who came up with a very long list of the characteristic features of the kind of lady he would like to marry. His list was indeed very funny.

1. The lady must have a minimum qualification of B.A. or B.Sc. degree.
2. The lady must not be fat.
3. She must be very tall, with straight legs.
4. She must have an excellent singing voice.

That was a clear description of what he wanted. It is interesting to know that, he actually got someone whom he felt met all the four conditions. He brought the lady to the pastor. His pastor had a lot of doubt about the lady. So he asked the brother, "Can you tell me what the Lord told you about this lady?" He tried to answer but he was not loud enough. His pastor asked him to go back and pray again to be sure of what God actually want him to do. When a pastor tells a member, to go and pray again, he is simply saying that the member must have made a mistake.

However, the brother came back and maintained that it was the same lady. The pastor could not persuade him to change his mind. The brother went ahead and married the lady. The wedding ceremony was highly successful by human standards.

Prayer Strategies for Singles

When they got home, the brother asked the wife to kneel down with him so that they can pray together. Both of them knelt down in their wedding dresses and the brother led the prayer, but the wife refused to say Amen. The brother stopped to ask her why she was not saying Amen. Her answer was shocking, "I don't want to say Amen. I don't want to have anything to do with the name of Jesus."

There was no going back for the brother. He had married a wife who was highly demonic. That brother's example, shows us that, all those who decide to claim whatever they like through blind faith must be prepared to face the consequence.

It is quite simple to say "I am not afraid of anything. The Bible has told me that wherever the sole of my feet shall tread, I shall possess." Well, that is true. But you can graduate from that level and become a believer who can say "O Lord, not my will but thy will be done." The brother met somebody who met all his conditions. He had his way. He failed, because he did not depend on the leadership of the Holy Spirit.

Do not depend on your own understanding, when it comes to the issue of the choice of a partner. If God decides, to give you the lady who does not appear to meet your requirements, it is better to accept God's will, than to go for somebody who will drink your blood. The devil knows that once he succeeds in making you take a wrong step, he has destroyed the foundation of your life. That is why he concentrates his energy on the initial approach.

He generally influences men and women to base their choices on lust or physical attraction. Most people have built their homes on the foundation of wild and foolish love.

Whenever a marriage is based on lust, age, or beauty, couples end up having problems when these things fade away. The forces of darkness employ the weapon of lust, infatuation, and demonic attraction. When such marriages are contracted, they end up becoming marriages of convenience.

Somebody phoned me from overseas saying, "Doctor Olukoya, I would like to inform you that there is someone who wants to marry me. But the problem with that man is that he is not worthy to be my husband. Do you think I should marry him?" I told her to think properly about the step she was about to take. I asked her, "What makes you think that you are the only one who wants to manage the man. What if the man is just trying to manage you also, both of you might end up managing each other." That kind of marriage cannot work.

Some people take blind steps into marriage. They come across a man, they don't even know where he lives, and they agree to follow the man to the marriage registry. People who pick themselves on the road in that manner, cannot experience a happy home. Also, all those who go into sex before marriage are building their homes on the foundation on failure. When any marriage is based on the principle of the forces of darkness, such a marriage will not last.

A secondary school student suddenly becomes pregnant and the parents force her to get married. That kind of marriage will surely not work. Very soon, they will part the way they met. If you are not led by the Spirit of God, your marriage can never be established on a solid foundation.

The issue of marriage has become the most difficult area of life in the African continent. Forces of darkness are attacking young people, by hindering them from getting married. We all know that powers of darkness are very active in the African society.

One of their major tasks is to ensure that no home is successful or peaceful. These forces begin their work right from the home. They attack bachelors and spinsters who want to get married. The moment they discover that someone has known the will of God in marriage, they try to frustrate and confuse such a person.

They also attack those who are yet to discover God's choice for them in marriage, by trying to influence such people to pick just anybody.

Those who have been settled in the area of choosing the right partner are not spared by satanic forces. They also make sure that they place stumbling blocks before them.

Prayer Strategies for Singles

That is why we often come across brothers and sisters who have made up their minds to marry each other, but cannot make any progress for two or three years.

Why is the devil doing all these? It is simply because he knows that the moment you succeed in the area of marriage, he would have lost a great battle. This matter is so weighty that I would like you to close your eyes right now and take these prayer points. This is not a prayer to be handled with levity. Psychedelic or academic prayers will not work in this area. You must pray fervently and with holy aggression. The only prayer that can destroy all the works of satan set up against your marriage is violent aggressive prayers done in violent faith.

- *Any evil power, that does not want to leave me alone, fall down and die, in the name of Jesus.*
- *Any household wickedness, that does not want to leave me alone, fall down and die, in Jesus' name.*

If you take these prayer points aggressively, a lot of things will be destroyed in the spiritual realm.

That the enemy is fighting against your own marriage needs no argument. You must therefore, seek to understand and identify the type of forces which he is using against you. If you are an African, you would have noticed that there are myriads of local forces which the devil uses to hinder people from getting married and to work against marriages that have already been established.

THE LOCAL FORCES
What then are these local forces?

• Collective captivity
This is a very powerful demonic force. How do you identify collective captivities? Whenever you see a family where every member is suffering from the same problem, such people are suffering from collective captivity.

I have come across cases, where each of the ladies from a particular family failed to get a husband. I have also seen cases where members of the same family who are men and are aged 35 years and above failed to find any woman who will accept marrying them. I have also seen families, where everyone who ever married ended up with divorce.

Again, I have seen families where all married couples were childless. That is an example of collective captivity.

If you know a particular family where there are three or four ladies who are mature and none of them is able to get anyone who has proposed marriage to her, then you must understand that they are suffering from collective captivity.

When you see sisters from the same parents who are 35, 40 and 42, and cannot get any one to marry them, then you are sure that there is a stubborn yoke, in that family. The problem is not limited to one member of the family, it is a general problem.

Let us look at a typical family. Sister Mary is the first born of the family, she is 42, and she is not married. Sister

Prayer Strategies for Singles

Joy is the second child, she got married, and was later divorced by the husband. Brother Keneth is the third child, he is 38 and has vowed not to marry until he comes across a Chinese sister who is born again. Incidentally, the brother who wants to marry a Chinese sister does not even have an international passport. The fourth member of the family is a lady, working on her Masters' degree. At 36, she has vowed never to marry until she has her Ph.D. degree. The last child of the family is 34 years old, he is a business man. He has told everyone that he would never think of getting married until he has made his millions. That was how everyone of them failed to get married as a result of flimsy excuses, and un-natural reasons.

Such people may never marry, except they went through deliverance, and secure divine intervention in their situations. Are you suffering from collective captivity?

A very wealthy woman once came to me with a very strange problem. She was married to a man who refused to do any work. The woman provides all the money needed to run the family. The man wakes up in the morning, takes his bath, and applies expensive perfume on his body. He dresses up, brushes his teeth and takes his breakfast. Then, he seats down throughout the whole day watching Television. He goes to sleep whenever he is tired. He doesn't do any business.

Funny enough, he calls his wife whenever it is Christmas time saying "Madam, do you want your husband to stay in the house without any money in his pocket. Give me some pocket money. Twenty or fifty thousand Naira will be O.K." The woman would write him a cheque because she was very rich. That was how the man became woman in his house and the woman the head of the family.

The woman became disturbed by the situation and decided to come to me for counselling and prayer. As I closed my eyes to pray for her, the Lord told me to stop praying and ask her some questions. Then I told her to sit down and answer some questions. The first question I asked her was:

"How many ladies are there in your family?"

"My mother had 8 daughters."

"Did your parents give birth to any male child?"

I probed further, "How many of your sisters are married?" "None", she answered, "I am the only one who is married."

Then I sat her down and made her to understand that she was suffering from collective captivity. I also told her that all the children of her parents were not supposed to get married at all. She had broken the rule, that was why her marriage was not working. I told her to go through deliverance, in order to break loose from her family's captivity. It was only at that point that it dawned on her that her husband's strange behavior was an off-shoot of the problem of her family.

If you are passing through this kind of situation, you cannot experience success in your marriage plans unless you identify and break the yoke that is responsible for the problems.

Something has continued to baffle me. There are cases of people who come to me for help, without being conscious of the depth of the problem which they were going through. I remember a particular case of a lady who came from a family of five. Everyone of them was suffering from collective captivity, except the only one who was born again. She was given some prayer points and told to pray in order to move herself away from underneath the evil umbrella.

Instead of going to pray, she said, "Excuse me pastor, I did not come to see you because of myself, I am concerned about the situation of the other members of the family. After all, my own problem is very small, when compared with that of other members of the family. The first born of the family is 50 years old, and he is not yet married. The second child is 45. She did not get married, she only managed to have a child for a married man. Why should I be so worried about myself. After all, I am only 33 years old. Why don't you talk about my other brothers and sister."

That was a very foolish approach. Even if we talk about the condition of members of the family who were not born again, they were not yet qualified to experience deliverance from collective captivity.

The way out of captivity is for members of the family who are already born again, to first get out of the bondage, before thinking of helping other people. If you decide to concentrate on the condition of unsaved members of your family you will end up prolonging your captivity. However, if all the members of the family are born again, the job becomes easier. All of you can get yourselves together, and declare war on the powers that are holding you captive.

- **Anti-marriage forces**

If you discover that your marriage is following the evil pattern of your parents in any way, then you need to fight against anti-marriage forces. If it happens that your father or mother could not really settle down in the family, and you are also finding it hard to sort out yourself in the area of marriage then you need to realize that something has been passed down to you. It is unlikely that the same anti-marriage forces which fought against your parents' home, are also at work in your own marriage.

You have probably inherited anti-marriage forces from your parents. You must pray against anti-marriage forces. Even if the anti-marriage forces are working against your life without your having inherited them, you must still fight against those wicked forces.

- **The travails of the first born**

In the African society, the first born is generally besieged on all fronts. This happens for a number of reasons.

One, the first born is often a target of attack. Enemies generally believe that the first born is the glory of the home. They believe that if they succeed in destroying the first born of the family, they have gotten the glory of that family. In some places, the first born of a family is dedicated or covenanted to family idols. Such an evil dedication, generally puts the first born into all kinds of troubles.

Besides, whenever parents have their first child, they normally take such babies to fetish priests for protection. Their purpose is to preserve the life of the first born. They also end up introducing problems into the life of such a baby.

Three, the first born in a large or polygamous families are often attacked by other children in the family. They do so in order to prevent the first born from claiming the father's inheritance. In some families, the father has many houses, lands, farms and other valuable properties. The other children, often gang up or fight individually against the first born. Whichever way you look at it, the first born of the family is generally under attack. That is why, it is often difficult for the first born to succeed in life. He receives most of the attacks that come into the family. This is the travail of the first born.

Unfortunately many first born have been used as human torches to clear the road for other members of the family. They carry the load of other children in the family. Other children in the family generally end up doing very well, while the first born remains useless to himself and to the family. You must break the yoke if you happen to be the first born of your parents.

Prayer Strategies for Singles

- **Spirit husband or spirit wife**

The problems of spirit wives or spirit husbands are universal. It is not limited to the African society. The spirit wives/husbands phenomenon is spiritual in nature. Hence, it knows no geographical boundary. It has become so popularised that the whites have given special names to it. They call them Incubus and Succubus. Spirit wives and spirit husbands operate in two ways.

The first method of operation involves the activity of real demons who come to people in the dream to excite and abuse them sexually. These powers forcefully marry their victims in the dream. The demons are so powerful that once they have taken somebody as their wives, they become very jealous. That is why some women die during childbirth. Their spirit husbands are jealous and will never allow them to give birth to children in real life.

A woman who has a spirit husband would find it very difficult to get married. In fact, the spirit husband will be so angry that he will attempt to deal with anyone who tries to share his wife with him.

The second category consists of wicked human spirits, who decide to use their power against you. The wicked satanic agents could be a man or a woman. Such a spirit wife or spirit husband comes across someone whom they admire. But, because they did not know what to do in real life they decide to use their evil powers to get what they want when their victims are unconscious. They simply transfer their spirits out of their bodies, take up the appearance of someone who is familiar with their victims and then go ahead to have sex with them.

They could put on the face of their fiance or fiancee, a respected friend, a relative or even a pastor in order not to attract suspicion or resistance. If the spirit husband or wife comes to you as a total stranger you are likely to resist the move. But you will probably give in if the appearance happens to be that of someone you have already accepted to get married to. By the time such wicked human beings have succeeded in having sex with you, they would have also transferred some evil poisons into your life.

You must therefore, destroy and paralyze every spirit husband or wife who attempts to destroy your chances of achieving a stable marriage.

I pity those who have sex in dreams and decide to ignore it. Such people discover that every plan they make towards getting married, ends up in failure and confusion. This is simply because the one to whom they are married in the spiritual realm has placed some embargo on their lives.

Don't tolerate any attack from spirit husbands or spirit wives. If you accommodate them by allowing them to constantly have sex with you in your dreams, you are allowing problems into your life in the area of marriage.

- **Financial curse**

A lot of people today are under the curse of poverty and

financial embarrassment. They work like elephants and eat like ants. They patch everything ranging from shoes to their dresses. Some people get to the point where the shoemaker becomes tired of mending their shoes, advising them to throw the shoes away and buy another one. Others have to beg before they can eat a meal. Some men who are praying about getting married have no accommodation of their own. Some of them sleep on a mat near their uncle's bed. If such a man finds a wife where will he make his home?

Financial curse can hinder a man from getting married. Whenever an evil power, wants to hinder a man from getting married, they will attack him with the curse of poverty, knowing that someone who is extremely poor will find it difficult to get married. This is one of the satanic weapons which have been used to make a lot of people to decide not to get married.

- **Bad family names**

Many people have tried very hard to get married, and have failed woefully. Their moves to get married have been checkmated by their evil family names. Some of these have demonic origin. Others are attached to a very powerful idol. If you have tried to get married without succeeding you should settle down to examine your family name. Have you thought about your family name? It could be the source of all the disappointments which you have had.

Many believers have experienced great things in their lives, immediately they decide to change their names.

Prayer Strategies for Singles

They discover that problems disappear as soon as they effect a change of name.

A woman once came to me because she had a strange dream. While she was sleeping, someone came to her with a double barrel gun. The strange personality looked at her and announced "Madam you are dying today." She was so fearful that she shouted "Jesus help me." Immediately, she found two sticks of broom beside her. She took up the two brooms and attempted to fight a man who was holding a gun. She woke up and shouted for help from the neighbour who helped her to my office for prayer. I had to interview her before praying about her problem. "Madam what is your name", I asked her? She answered "Sir, my name is Sobote."

If you understand Yoruba language you will understand that her name is pregnant with meaning. It simply means 'wizard gave birth to rebellion.' That was the meaning of her name. Tell me how won't such a name work against her. She was living under the heavy load of the consequences of rebellion and witchcraft.

If your name is *Sangobiyi*, which means *Sango* (the idol of thunder) gave birth to you or *Esubiyi*, which means *Esu* (the most wicked demonic deity in Yoruba mythology) gave birth to you, then you can be sure that something is wrong somewhere.

An Ibo man came to me, sometime ago, for prayer and deliverance. When I asked to know his name I became shocked when he told me that his name means darkness in

60

Igbo language. Such a man will experience a lot of darkness in his life. Should he continue to bear such a name? You must get rid of evil names. You should settle down to examine your family name. You must cancel every unprofitable name if you want to make progress in your marriage.

• **Satanic marks**

Here, I refer to invisible marks. I know people who are followed by evil marks everywhere they go. Whenever they lay their hands on anything, they meet with failure. Bachelors and spinsters who have evil marks in their lives often experience marital failure.

Ladies have become helpless victims of satanic marks. When such ladies come across a man who promises to get married to them, they go ahead to make wonderful plans, only to be surprised to discover a sudden or drastic change in the attitude of the man, who was once loving and sweet.

Something happened in France recently. A lady was brought to the court and charged for indecent assault. What actually happened was that, she had been engaged to a man who suddenly decided that he was not going to have anything to do with the lady again. She made two thousand telephone calls to the house of the man who jilted her within 24 hours. The man became tired of being inundated with embarrassing telephone calls and dragged her to court. That was how the lady was sentenced to imprisonment.

Unknown to the lady, there was an evil mark in her life.

That was why the man was no longer interested in her. If you have discovered that, everyone who has promised to get married to you ends up changing their minds, you must realize that there is an evil mark upon your life. You must get this evil mark erased through the blood of Jesus.

When men, who are having evil marks upon their lives come across women who will profit them, they would avoid such women and go for those who will give them problems. That is an evidence of having an evil mark.

● **The Spirit Of Rejection**
The problems of many people, who have had difficulties in the area of identifying, choosing and getting married to the right partner, stem from the fact that they are attacked by the spirit of rejection. Whenever you see a bachelor or a spinster who is afraid of getting married as a result of the fear of having a bad marriage, then you can be sure that such a person has decided to carry the rejection which he or she suffered in the past into the future.

Some people, do not have any good memory concerning their past lives.

Those who were hated, abused and maltreated by their parents or guardians generally find it difficult to believe that they can ever have a stable home.

Those whose fathers or mothers were very wicked to them, generally find it difficult to trust anyone.

If you examine the lives of those who have negative

attitudes to life, you would have discovered that such people never experienced any form of parental love. Such people, generally started out in life with a bad foundation. Maybe, when they were young, they lost their parents and had to live with some wicked uncles who treated them as if they were not human beings.

Maybe they went from the house of such wicked uncles, to live with their grandmothers. By the time they tell you the number of places they had lived, you will come up with ten or so places. When you interview them, they would tell you that they believe that nobody on earth loves them. Such people are generally introverts. A very powerful spirit of rejection had settled in their lives.

With that background, facing the future will be difficult. Such people, need to receive deliverance from the spirit of rejection.

● **Parental Curses**

Parents generally curse their children as if such curses do not really mean anything. When a child makes a mistake, parents often make statement like "Your child will do to you what you have done unto me." That is a very terrible curse.

Many mothers and fathers curse their children in moments of anger. They make statements like "You will never experience peace in your home." "You will never settle down in your own home." "None of your children will ever listen to you because you refused to listen to me." "You will never make it in life. Everything you will lay your hands upon, will end up with failure. You will only succeed in life if you did not suck my breast."

Such powerful curses have worked against the lives of so many people today.

The truth is that our parents have authority over us. Their curses can work upon our lives if we fail to cancel every parental curse which has been placed upon your life since you were born.

- ## Bad Health

A lot of people experience marital failure because of bad health. There are people who always become sick each time they come up with serious plans in the area of marriage. What do you think would happen, when a man decides to get married to a lady and discovers that the lady is always sick? The man would think of running for his dear life, in order to avoid taking care of a sicklier all the days of his life.

There are people, who always fall sick mysteriously, whenever they come across a decent partner. This kind of sickness is not normal. It is generally ochestrated by powers that hinder marriage. Nobody wants to marry sicklier. Satanic agents are always active in manipulating the health conditions of those who want to get married.

A sister once narrated a strange experience to me. She had taken her fiance to her father who happened to be a serious demonic agent. The father specifically instructed them to go for blood test in a particular clinic.

64

Unknown to her, the father was looking for ways of rejecting her fiancee. He had connived with the doctor of that clinic who was a member of the same cult. His goal was to give them an evil clinical prophecy. I therefore advised an them to go to a popular Nigerian University College Hospital, a place that is respected for medical laboratory tests.

They followed my instructions to the letter and came back with a favourable result. When they gave the result of the blood test to the girl's father, he screamed at them asking them why they decided to avoid the particular clinic which he chose. They simply told him that they did the test at a renown university hospital. The father felt disappointed, but there was nothing he could do. His satanic plan failed woefully.

Don't allow the devil to manipulate your health condition and set it up as a stumbling block on the road to your marriage.

● Spiritual Dowry

Just as bride price is important in the physical realm, it is also important in the spiritual realm.

What then does a spiritual dowry mean?

The payment of spiritual dowry takes place in the spiritual realm. If you have a wicked mother or grandmother, who belongs to the spirit world, such a parent, may decide to give out your hand in marriage and collect your bride price in the spiritual realm. That means that, you have been married in the spiritual realm.

65

Generally, the fact that a dowry has been paid by a personality in the spiritual realm means that you have already got married. It will be difficult, therefore, to find anyone who will accept to get married to you in real life.

Unfortunately, most people are not aware of the payment of such a dowry. Therefore they make several efforts in order to get married but every effort fails, because their parents have collected the bride price in the spiritual realm. Nobody will ever come up to pay any dowry on such a person. This is one of the local forces which cause problems in marriages in the African environment.

- **Anti-maintenance Forces**

This local evil forces, will allow you to start a relationship but will never allow you to maintain the relationship. The problem of most people is that they are very quick to start new relationships, but they don't know how to keep the relationship going. This is the work of anti-maintenance forces.

- **The Spirit Of Polygamy**

This spirit, is prevalent in almost every African community. It is a common knowledge that most African families are polygamous in nature. This is not an ordinary thing. There is a spirit behind it. When this kind of spirit, comes upon a woman, she will never find a man who has never married before to marry her. All those who propose marriage to her, are all married. All of them are inviting her to become second or third wife.

Prayer Strategies for Singles

A man who has the anointing of polygamy will never be satisfied with one woman. Although he has one or two wives at home, he will still be busy roaming about like a foolish dog. This kind of men are capable of doing a lot of unimaginable things. They can sleep with a woman everyday throughout the month without getting tired. Some pastors who belong to this category and fail to go through deliverance have fallen flat on their faces because the single wife which they have at home cannot cope with their excessive demand for sex.

● **Evil Marriage Covenant**

A lot of people have gone into evil marriage covenant, without being conscious of it. Unknown to such people, they have been donated to certain powers or shrines.

If you are in this category, you are already covenanted. You will find it difficult or impossible to break loose and live your own life.

● **Broken Homes**

If your parents are divorced or separated, you have a lot of prayers to pray. Those who come from broken homes, often find it difficult to achieve marital stability.

You must shield your own marriage from such evil influences. It has been observed that most of the people who come from broken homes often suffer the problem of marital instability themselves.

● **Homosexuality And Lesbianism**

This is a very stubborn force, which fight against people's efforts, towards getting married. The problem of homosexualism and lesbianism is not only restricted to the western world, it has also become common in Africa. If you attended a boarding house meant for boys or girls only, you would have discovered that it is generally common for girls to try to behave to other girls as if they were men. They often try to use many methods to give themselves some ungodly pleasure.

These twins' sins constitute a gross violation of Biblical principles. You must also deal with this problem if it is present in your life, or if you have ever got involved with it in the past.

You must deal with all these local forces, if you want your journey into marriage to be smooth, and if you want your marriage to work.

Deal with every local marriage scorpion today. Pray until all the hindrances to getting married successfully are consumed with the fire of the Holy Ghost. Subject all marriage scorpions to the fire of aggressive warfare prayers.

Your testimony is sure, in Jesus' name.

CHAPTER THREE
POWER AGAINST MARRIAGE SERPENTS

We do a great deal of praying during our services because we are aware of the fact that, it takes warfare to overcome in life. The forces, that are fighting against man, are so numerous that nobody can succeed in life without praying. The Bible says, "Pray without ceasing" (I Thess. 5:17).

I have discovered that, of all the activities that are carried out in the church, prayer is the only one that the devil cannot duplicate. Praise worship is good, but it does not constitute any threat to the devil. After all, he was formally the chief choir master in heaven.

The greatest musical talents in history have always belonged to the devil. One of such talented musicians recently spent his entire life serving the devil. He married more than twenty five wives. Surprisingly, he started out as a church organist. Both his father and grand father were Reverend gentlemen but the man later decided to serve the devil. According to newspaper reports, he died of AIDS. He was very talented, a sort of prodigy, yet he lived a wasted life.

I wonder what could have happened if he had devoted his life to the service of God. All these make us to know that music, church activities, social interaction among church members, preaching and other church programmes cannot replace prayers.

Prayer Strategies for Singles

Prayer is the only spiritual exercise with which we can fight the battles of life.

There is a very instructive and interesting story in The Acts of the Apostles chapter 28. Let us look at the first verse. "And when they were escaped, then they knew that the island was called Melita." Let me give you some background concerning this story.

The above statement was made by Paul. Paul and other people have been inside the ship for weeks. He had warned them at the outset of the voyage, but they ignored his warnings. A problem arose when they got to the middle of the sea. Things became so bad that they could not catch a glimpse of the sun. So, they decided to throw their goods into the sea. Despite this effort for the safety of the ship, their lives were still in jeopardy.

The situation got so bad, that they could not eat as a result of fear. They were without food for fourteen days. Paul later encouraged them to eat. He assured them that none of them was going to die. He used the opportunity to share the gospel with everyone in the ship. They finally got to Melita Island.

Now, let us look at verses 2-3, "And the Barbarous people showed us no little kindness. For they kindled fire and received us, everyone because of the present rain and because of the cold. And when Paul had gathered a bundle of sticks and laid them on the fire, there came a viper out of the heat and fastened on his hand."

We have a lot of lessons to learn from what happened to

Paul here. Here is a man who has had lots of troubles and trials. They have survived a deadly tidal wave. The ship wreck which would have claimed the lives of Paul and the others, brought them safely to an island. Now the devil wanted to disgrace him but the Lord disappointed the enemy. It would have been terrible if the last chapter of the book of Acts had ended with the death of Paul through the sting of the viper.

"And when the Barbarians saw the venomous beast hung on his hand, they said among themselves, no doubt this man is a murderer who though he had escaped the sea, yet vengeance suffered not to live."

Had he died at that time, his life would have ended as a bad testimony. Something wonderful happened in verse 5, "He shook off the beast into the fire and felt no harm. Howbeit they looked when he should have swollen or fallen down dead suddenly. But after they had looked a great while and saw no harm come to him, they changed their minds and said that he was a god."

And from that Island, Paul began to preach. The disgrace which the enemy planned for Paul was eventually turned to disgrace for the enemy.

Perhaps, you share the same experience with Paul. You might have a viper on your own hands. Of course, this may not be a physical viper. May be the enemy has fastened the viper of anger, malice or unforgiving spirit. The purpose of these vipers is to destroy God's plan for your life. You must be ready to fight a good fight of faith. God will give you the victory just as He granted Paul victory. Get ready, you will soon shake the viper into the fire.

These vipers represent marriage serpents. You must not spare any of them. You must throw them into the fire, where they belong.

Jesus made an outstanding statement in Mark 16:18, "They shall take up serpents; and if they drink any deadly thing, it shall not hurt them. They shall lay their hands on the sick and they shall recover."

This is an amazing promise. This verse assures us, that no serpent and scorpion shall hurt us.

I want you to close your eyes right now and take this powerful prayer point.

● *I shake off, every spiritual serpent, fastened to my hand, in the name of Jesus.*

MARRIAGE SERPENTS

What are marriage serpents? We need to take a close look at these satanic forces in order to identify, destroy and expel them from our lives. If you can destroy the activities of these marriage serpents, you will experience success in every step on your way.

The marriage journey of most people have been aborted as a result of these serpentine forces.

● **Human Beings**

Human beings constitute a .very wicked serpentine force. The Bible says: "The wicked are like poisonous serpents, malicious and tricky." This group of people attack marriages. They constitute themselves into stumbling blocks and stand in the way of those who want to marry.

Human beings, either they are your relatives or not, will try to attack your marriages. A lot of people think that they have mothers or fathers but they don't have parents in the real sense of the word.

Some mothers are behind the problems of late marriages in the lives of their children.

Two sisters flew in from England having heard of what God is doing at the Mountain of Fire and Miracles. The first was thirty-nine, while the second one was thirty seven, but they were unmarried. They decided to come and see me and go through deliverance in order to put an end to the problem of remaining single at old age. The Lord gave me a revelation immediately the two of them sat down before me. That happened at the end of their deliverance programme.The Lord told me that their father was responsible for what they were going through, but I found it difficult to tell them.

I threw a question at them. "Where are you going from here?" "Oh we will just say hello to daddy", they chorused. Then I warned them saying, "Make sure that you do not allow him to embrace you." They said but that's normal. "He would kiss and embrace us." I told them to keep a distance from their dad, if not, the deliverance they had gone through would be nullified. The London ladies looked at me in a strange manner.

"But why shouldn't we embrace our daddy?", they asked. I warned them once again: "I don't know if you have a daddy or not. If you allow him to embrace you, you will be back to square one."

Immediately they got home, their father wanted to embrace them but they moved backward and said, "Daddy, we are going back right away. This is what we brought for you." They handed over the parcel and turned back. "Wait! Wait!" said their father. "Why are you moving away from me. Okay, I know what happened. You went to that church and they told you not to allow me to embrace you. You think I didn't know where you went." That was how the two ladies rushed back to my office and narrated their experiences.

One of them said, "Pastor, I didn't believe when you asked us not to allow our daddy to embrace us. I wouldn't have believed anything if things did not happen this way." They did not know that each time their father embraced them, men who would have married them were driven away mysteriously. That shows us that there are wicked fathers.

I heard a story of the father who bought a cemetery for all his children. Whenever each of them died he made sure that he personally provided the money for the coffin. What a wicked father! Why should parents use evil powers to prevent their children from getting married?

Prayer Strategies for Singles

There are many reasons behind that kind of wicked action. Some mothers are envious of their daughters.

A man became angry because his children were attending our church. He decided to come and attack me. He came well prepared, with a very powerful charm in his pocket. His intention was to get rid of me as soon as he succeeded in shaking hands with me. Incidentally, the Lord had revealed to me everything he was doing. Immediately he brought out his hand from his pocket, I stretched forward my hands to shake him. Instead of removing my hand from his, I kept it there and looked straight into his eyeballs and said, "I think you don't know where you are. Do you think that you can eliminate me through ordinary shaking of hands? Do you think that if that kind of charm can affect me, I will still be here? You are a small boy. Jesus Christ is the greater one. If I wanted to deal with you, I will simply command the charm in your pocket to begin to attack you." He started shivering and went down on his face to beg, saying "I am sorry sir."

Human beings can become serpents. A lady came across a responsible wealthy man and brought him to her parents to seek for their approval. A family meeting was called and the members of the family who were demonic tried to reject the man. Their purpose was to prevent the lady from getting a good husband. They told her to bring someone from their village. When the lady complained saying, "Most of the men in our village are poor and illiterate", they instructed her to get just anybody from the village. At the end, the lady was confused. These are parts of the strategies of marriage serpents.

Members of your family may drive away the best husband from you.

I remember the story of a sister who found a wonderful brother and decided to take him to her family. Immediately they got home, the members of her family looked at him scornfully. That was how the man, concluded that he was not wanted by the family of the sister. Their intention was to drive the man away. This they achieved, as their action spoke louder than their voice. The sister's parents were serpents who did not want her to get a good choice in marriage.

Do you know that friends and acquaintances can also turn themselves into serpents and drive away good prospective husbands or wives from you? Such people will try to discourage you by making bad comments concerning your partner.

● **Materials That Are Laden With Spiritual Power**

A lot of materials which look ordinary on the surface could be terribly demonized. Such materials or objects can work against your marriage. People think that rings, earrings, bangles and chains are ordinary objects. They do not see any danger in them. What I normally tell people is that until they get to a point where they are able to discern whether a piece of ornamental metal is bewitched or demonic, they should avoid using such delicate items as a way of avoiding bondage.

Even if you want to be selective in the type of jewellery you want to use, how do you know which one is demonic and which one is not?

● **Sleeping With Satanic Agents**

A lot of people have invited terrible problems into their lives in the area of marriage, by having sex with demonic agents. Unknown to most ladies, the sex organs of some satanic agents who appear as innocent men are serpent's tails. The sex organ of some women are nothing but serpent's mouths. Therefore, if a person makes the mistake of sleeping with such demonic ladies or men, they are in a big trouble.

If you have mistakenly run into such a serpentine trap, in the past, you must go through deliverance. I pity ladies and men who decide to walk into such traps even after they have known the Lord. Such people will suffer greatly. The moment you have any sexual relationship with satanic agents, they will inject some poisons into your life. The poison will be used to drive away those who will make good husbands or wives from them.

THE NATURE OF SERPENTS

You need to study the nature of serpents if you want to know how to deal with them. If you want your arrow to hit the target, you must know the nature and the workings of

77

a serpent. Let us therefore look at the characteristics briefly.

• **Serpents Enjoy Living In Dark Holes**

Serpents are very active, in dark places. Maybe, you are the type who is fond of staying in dark places, you may not be far away from the abode of serpents.

Disco addicts and those who keep late nights as well as those who enjoy the company of strange men and women, invite serpents into their lives. It means that the aroma of dark holes is still in you. Such people, would find it difficult to find a partner simply because the mark of the serpent's hole is upon their lives.

All forms of spiritual darkness, invite serpents to peoples' lives. Ladies and men who fall into this category are always confused.

• **Serpents Move Craftily**

Serpents are very tricky and dangerous. Some ladies and men come across partners who are snaky in character. Such people strike suddenly and run away. Once they bite their victims, they run away looking for the next victim.

• **Serpents Are Sometimes Very Quiet And Unnoticed Before Striking Their Victims**

They normally destroy their victims suddenly. This kind of people are filled with 'kill-and-go-spirit'. Many men, who fall into this category, disguise as quiet men only to strike at the appropriate moment.

There are women, who put on the garment of

innocence, only to strike wickedly at the appropriate time.

• **Serpents Lay Eggs**

Spiritual serpents lay destructive eggs of sin in peoples' lives. These eggs are in the form of pride, arrogance, spiritual darkness, mind blockage, lack of concentration in Bible study and prayer, sleeping during prayer, dejection, depression and sadness.

When marriage serpents, succeed in laying these eggs, they end up bringing problems into the lives of people.

DESTROYING MARRIAGE SERPENTS

Finally, let us look at steps to be taken to destroy marriage serpents. These steps are very important. If you succeed in taking them, you will experience victory over all marriage serpents.

• **Learn To Listen To God**

Man is naturally deaf. All seeds of Adam are born deaf and dumb. You must learn, how to listen to God with quietness in your heart. That is why I have always said that, the greatest recipe for failure is to refuse to hear from God. You get into trouble by not hearing what God wants you to do concerning your marriage.

Every effort made, in learning to listen to God properly, is not wasted. The more you hear God speaking to you, the more you will enjoy every step taken in the area of marriage.

A lot of people will save themselves unnecessary

79

problems and heartaches, if only they can hear from God. If you fail to listen to God, you will spend your entire life fighting battles. A good army general knows that spending the whole of one's life fighting battles is a sheer waste of time.

You must know what God wants you to do at all times.

● **Avoid Sin**

Sin is the food for the serpent. As long as sin is found in your life, it will continue to come to you. Sin attracts serpents to people's lives. Steer clear from sin. Don't be like the proverbial person whose enemies are trying to roast and he decides to apply petrol on himself as body cream. Such a person is simply facilitating the entire process.

If a serpent wants to attack a person's marriage and the person mistakenly falls into sin, the person will suffer terribly. There are some people who say that they can go ahead and commit sin and quickly ask God for mercy. Such people are deceiving themselves. They have forgotten that the Bible says, "I will have mercy on whom I will have mercy." That shows that it is not automatic, that everyone who asks for mercy receives it.

● **Get Rid Of Every Trace Of Fear In Your Life**

If Paul had been fearful when the snake fastened itself upon his hand, he would have been defeated by the devil.

Parents generally instil fear into their children.

Some ladies and men who are still single, are under

tremendous pressure from their parents. Their parents tell them lots of things that make them to be afraid.

A lot of people made wrong choices, because they were living under morbid fear and anxiety. I normally tell people that the devil is afraid of fearless people.

• **Be Filled With The Holy Ghost**

Serpents will have no power over you if you are always filled with the Spirit. You will be too hot for them to handle.

• **Pray In The Spirit**

Spirit filled praying, is poisonous to serpents. If you can form the habit of praying in the spirit at all times, serpents will not be able to bite you. In fact, they will keep a distance from your life.

• **Destroy All Serpentine Influences**

Pray them away from your life. Get rid of all snaky influences. Many people rely on doctor's report as if they are divine verdicts. All such influences must be dealt with.

• **Possess The Hands of Fire**

When your hands are filled with power, a serpent will never be able to fasten itself on them.

You can deal with all these problems if you take the above steps. Your marriage is a possibility. Once you are ready to obey the word of God and pray aggressively, you will go through the process of knowing the will of God, getting married and raising a happy family, without any ugly interruption from wicked serpents. Pray, until every marriage serpent is destroyed.

PRAYER SECTION

BREAKING ANTI-MARRIAGE YOKE

**Spend some quality time to praise and worship
God before you pray these prayer points.**

1. Worship the Lord and thank Him for His unfailing good promises ... and what He has promised, He is able to perform (1 Kings 8:56, Rom. 7:21).
2. Thank God for His rainbow of unfailing promises: for His Word in Him is yes and amen. (2Cor.1:20).
3. Praise God for His exceeding great and precious promises for your life (2 Pet. 1:4).
4. Confess all your sins to God, ask for forgiveness and pray for mercy.
5. Holy Spirit, energize me to pray to the point of breakthroughs, in Jesus' name.
6. (Lay your right hand on your head) Fire of God, charge my body, soul and spirit, in Jesus' name.
7. Pray in this song: There is power mighty in the blood (2ce), there is power mighty in the blood of Jesus Christ, there is power mighty in the blood.
8. Blood of Jesus, .   .   .
   i) Flow into my foundation and cleanse out every evil design
   ii) rob off, every evil mark of anti-marriage from my life
   iii) Nullify, every evil spiritual agreement I have made with the spirit husband/wife consciously or unconsciously

iv) rob off, every contrary handwriting that is against my life

v) Flush out, every evil dream food and poisons from my root.

9. Sing these songs
   i) Holy Ghost fire, fire fall on me, like the day of Pentecost, fire fall on me.
   ii) Holy Ghost, arise in Your power (2ce), Ready to deliver, ready to save . . .

10. Cover yourself with the blood of Jesus and pray thus:
    i) Holy Ghost fire, fall on me, burn in my body, soul and spirit, in Jesus' name.
    ii) Fire of God, go down to my root and burn every evil worm eating up God's plan for my life, in the name of Jesus.
    iii) By the blood of Jesus, I break every evil spiritual marriage vow.
    vi) By the blood of Jesus, I cut myself, off from every evil spiritual marriage vow.
    v) In the name of Jesus, I withdraw myself, from the evil association of . . . (pick from the underlisted).
       a) the unmarried   b) late marriages
       c) the bewitched   d) God's enemies
       e) the self-afflicted f) zero catchers
    vi) I break, every evil vow, by my parents on my behalf, in the name of Jesus.

11. I denounce every evil association of . . . (pick from the underlisted), in the name of Jesus.
    - familiar spirit   - water spirit

Prayer Strategies for Singles

- getting married in the dream   - witches
- wizards   - sorcerers
- wandering about in the dream
- star gazers, etc (mention any other ones you know you are involved)

12. Strange marks on my life, be robbed off by the blood of Jesus.
13. I break, every barrier between me and my partner, in the name of Jesus.
14. I reject, every evil family pattern, in Jesus' name.
15. Blood of Jesus, arrow of God's deliverance, deliver me now from . . . (pick from the underlisted), in the name of Jesus.
    a) spirit of late marriage   b) spirit of error
    c) spirit of disappointment   d) spirit of loneliness
16. O Lord, open Your book of remembrance to my page now, in the name of Jesus.
17. I plead the blood of Jesus, over my life and this environment, in the name of Jesus.
18. Every power, of the prince of Persia, blocking my prayers all these years, fall down and die, in the name of Jesus.
19. In the name of Jesus, by the blood of Jesus, I release myself from . . . (pick from the underlisted)
    - any form of parental curse placed on me consciously or unconsciously
    - evil effect of placenta bondage

- spirit husband / wife
- self imposed curses
- the spirit of non-achievement
- garment of shame and reproach
- yearly sorrows
- Periodic disappointments

20. In the name of Jesus, I denounce every
    - evil spiritual marriage
    - association with familiar spirits
    - association with witchcraft/wizard spirit
    - membership of the dark-world
    - association with God's enemies

21. O Lord, by the blood of Jesus, wash away my reproach, in the name of Jesus.

22. Any power, that will attack me, as a result of this prayer programme, fall down and die, in Jesus' name

23. In the name of Jesus, by the fire of the Holy Ghost, I reject. . .
    i) every evil prophecy of late marriage on my life
    ii) every spirit of getting married in the dream
    Iii) every garment of shame and reproach
    iv) every evil voice, speaking defeat into my ears
    v) every spiritual marriage certificate, signed in the spirit world on my behalf, to nullify my marriage here on earth

24. This very day, in the name of Jesus, I shall . . .
    i) receive my deliverance
    ii) receive my breakthroughs
    iii) receive joy instead of sadness
    iv) receive the touch of God
    v) receive divine solution to my life's problem
    vi) laugh last, my enemies shall cry
25. O Lord, rend the heavens, and send down help for me, in the name of Jesus.
26. You root of impossibilities, working against my life, be uprooted, in the name of Jesus.
27. Anything, making the promise of God, to fail in my life, receive the thunder fire of God, and be roasted, in the name of Jesus.
28. I break, every curse of automatic marital failure, working in my family, in the name of Jesus.
29. Father Lord, destroy every circle of problem in my life, in the name of Jesus.
30. I cancel, every bewitchment fashioned against my marital life, in the name of Jesus.
31. Let all anti-marriage marks, be removed with the blood of Jesus, in the name of Jesus.
32. I Ignite, the foundation of my marriage programme, with the liquid fire of God, in the name of Jesus.
33. Let every satanic agent, assigned against my marital life, be afflicted with the wrath of God, in Jesus name

34. Every legal ground, of household wickedness, against my desired marital life, receive the thunder fire of God and be consumed to ashes, in Jesus' name.
35. I break and deliver myself with the blood of the Lamb from any conscious or unconscious demonic covenanted marriage, in the name of Jesus.
36. I withdraw, my marriage programme, from the prison of anti-marriage forces, in Jesus' name.
37. You spirit of late marriage, be located by the angels of the living God and be suffocated, in Jesus' name.
38. I break, every conscious or unconscious covenant I have entered into with the strong-man of late marriage, in the name of Jesus.
39. I refuse to accept satanic delay tactics, over my marriage, in the name of Jesus.
40. Anything, present in my life, that is anti-marriage, receive the liquid fire of God and melt away, in the name of Jesus.
41. I paralyse, every satanic manipulator, in the name of Jesus.
42. I paralyse, every evil trend in my life, in the name of Jesus.
43. I paralyse, every satanic incantation against my life, in the name of Jesus.
44. Every expectation, desire and device of the devil over my life, will not prosper, in the name of Jesus.

45. Let the angel of the Lord, pour liquid fire, on every spirit of witchcraft, militating against my life, in the name of Jesus.

46. Let the power, of every persistent, attacker dry up, in the name of Jesus.

47. Father Lord, shine Your light, into every area of my life and chase out every contrary thing, in the name of Jesus.

48. Oh Lord, magnetize my divinely ordained partner to me and keep all the others away.

49. Any hidden thing in my life, hindering the manifestation of my home, receive the fire of God, in Jesus' name.

50. Every satanic device, to delay my marriage programme, be rendered impotent, in Jesus' name.

51. Lord Jesus, establish my marriage this year to Your own glory, in the name of Jesus.

52. Father Lord, let my enemies congratulate me before the end of this year, in the name of Jesus.

53. I seal my victory with the blood of Jesus.

54. Right now, Holy Father, let Your 'sword of deliverance' touch my blood, in the name of Jesus.

55. Angels of the living God, search the land of the living and the land of the dead, and gather all fragmented parts of my life together, in the name of Jesus.

56. Pick from the under listed, and pray thus: Every ....,

operating in my life, against my marriage, fall down and die, in Jesus' name.
- spirit of the valley
- spirit of the tail
- spirit of the desert
- spirit of bitterness
- spirit of lateness in marriage
- spirit of shame and reproach
- spirit of loneliness
- spirit of unprogressive life

57. Pick from the under listed, and pray thus: Any ground that I have lost to the enemies through..., be withdrawn, in Jesus' name.
- sexual perversion
- telling lies
- fornication in the heart
- idolatry
- sex outside marriage
- abortion
- sale of virginity to strange men/women
- masturbation
- having sex with animals or objects
- coveting other people's husbands / wives

58. O Lord, make a way for me in this programme, in the name of Jesus.

59. O grave, where is thy victory? You could not hold back the Lord Jesus Christ. You will not hold back my breakthroughs, in the name of Jesus.

60. In this programme, O Lord, let me receive Your divine mercy and favour, in the name of Jesus.

61. By Your zeal O God of performance, carry out Your strange work and Your strange act in my life and surprise me greatly (Isa. 28: 21^b), in Jesus' name.

62. O God of new beginnings, do a new thing in my life, on this issue of marriage, and let every eye see it, in the name of Jesus.

63. Place your hand on any part of your body that you have sold off to strange men/women through immorality and pray thus: Sword of the Lord's deliverance, touch my (mention it), in Jesus' name.

64. Lay your hand on your head, and pray with this song: *Holy Ghost fire, fire fall on me, like the day of Pentecost, fire fall on me.*

65. I plead the blood of Jesus, over my life and this environment, in the name of Jesus.

66. Every power, of the Prince of Persia, blocking my prayers, all these years, fall down and die, in the name of Jesus.

67. In the name of Jesus, by the blood of Jesus, I release myself from . . . (pick from the under listed)
    - any form of parental curse, placed on me consciously or unconsciously
    - evil effect of placental bondage
    - spirit husband / wife
    - self imposed curses
    - the spirit of non-achievement
    - garment of shame and reproach
    - yearly sorrows
    - periodic disappointments

68. In the name of Jesus, I denounce every
    - evil spiritual marriage
    - association with familiar spirits
    - association with witchcraft/wizard spirit
    - membership of the dark-world
    - association with God's enemies

69. O Lord, by the blood of Jesus, wash away my reproach, in the name of Jesus.

70. Any power, that will attack me as a result of this prayer programme, fall down and die, in the name of Jesus.

71. Cover yourself with the blood of Jesus and pray thus:
    i) Holy Ghost fire, fall on me, burn in my body, soul and spirit, in the name of Jesus.
    ii) Fire of God, go down to my root, and burn every evil worm, eating up God's plan for my life, in the name of Jesus.
    iii) By the blood of Jesus, I break every evil spiritual marriage vow, in the name of Jesus.
    vi) By the blood of Jesus, I cut myself off, from every evil spiritual marriage vow, in the name of Jesus.
    v) In the name of Jesus, I withdraw myself from the evil association of ... (pick from the under listed).
       - the unmarried   - late marriages
       - the bewitched

Prayer Strategies for Singles

- God's enemies   - the self-afflicted
- none achievers

Vi) I break, every evil vow, by my parents on my behalf, in the name of Jesus.

72. I denounce, every evil association of . . . (pick from the under listed), in the name of Jesus.
    - familiar spirits   - water spirits
    - getting married in the dream
    - witches   - wizards   - sorcerers
    - wandering about in the dream
    - star gazers, etc (mention any other ones you know you are involved in)

73. Strange marks on my life, be robbed off by the blood of Jesus, in the name of Jesus.

74. I break, every barrier, between me and my partner, in Jesus' name.

75. I reject, every evil family pattern, in Jesus' name.

76. Blood of Jesus, arrow of God's deliverance, deliver me now from . . . (pick from the under listed), in the name of Jesus.
    - spirit of late marriage   - spirit of error
    - spirit of disappointment   - spirit of loneliness

77. O Lord, open Your book of remembrance for me now, in the name of Jesus.

78. I reject, devil's counterfeit, I receive God's original today, in the name of Jesus.

79. I reject and renounce every anti-marriage curses issued on me by my parents, in the name of Jesus.

80. In the name of Jesus, I command the strong East Wind of God to blow away, every distraction and hindrance often used by satan to block my partner, in Jesus' name.

81. In this programme, O Lord, I divorce my own will to receive God's will, in the name of Jesus.

82. By Your zeal O God of Jeshurun, send help to me, in Jesus' name.

83. Thou God of performance, do that which no man can do for me, in the name of Jesus.

84. By the blood of Jesus, I nullify every dream of ... (pick from the under listed).
    - swimming in the water   - eating strange food
    - drinking coke and fanta
    - having sex with fair or dark women / men
    - running without getting to a stop
    - talking alone without response
    - getting married with dirty garment
    - having children or breast-feeding
    - having bald head or hair falling off
    - sitting on a broken or cracked fence
    - falling inside the mud
    - eating inside a broken plate
    - getting married without wedding suit / dress
    - sleeping / playing in an uncompleted building

85. Every satanic wedding ring, be roasted, in the name of Jesus.

86. In the name of Jesus, every spirit of . . . (pick from the under listed) troubling my life, I reject, I renounce you and I command you to leave me now. By the blood of Jesus, I place the cross of the Lord Jesus Christ between me and you, and I forbid you to ever return to me.
    - mammy water
    - familiar spirit
    - unholy thought
    - wallowing in sins
    - unforgiveness
    - seduction   - Delilah
    - jealousy
    - high mindedness
    - husband / wife snatching
    - sexual thoughts
    - Jezebel

87. Lay your right hand on your head and pray:
    Fire of God, charge my body, soul and spirit, in the name of Jesus.

88. Holy Spirit, energize me to pray to the point of breakthroughs, in the name of Jesus.

89. Pray with this song: *There is power mighty in the blood (2x), there is power mighty in the blood of Jesus Christ, there is power mighty in the blood.*

90. Blood of Jesus, . . .
    - flow into my foundation and cleanse out every evil design

- rob off every evil mark of anti-marriage from my life
- nullify every evil spiritual agreement I have made with the spirit husband/wife consciously or unconsciously
- rob off every contrary handwriting, that is against my life
- flush out, every evil dream food and poison from my root.

91. In the name of Jesus, by the fire of the Holy Ghost, I reject . . .
   - every evil prophecy, of late marriage on my life
   - every spirit of getting married in the dream
   - every garment of shame and reproach
   - every evil voice, speaking defeat into my ears
   - every spiritual marriage certificate signed in the spirit world on my behalf to nullify my marriage here on earth

92. This very day, in the name of Jesus, I shall . . .
   - receive my deliverance
   - receive my breakthroughs
   - receive joy, instead of sadness
   - receive the touch of God
   - receive divine solution to my life's problem
   - laugh last. My enemies shall cry

93. O Lord, rend the heavens, and send down help for me, in the name of Jesus.

FREEDOM FROM INORDINATE AFFECTIONS AND SOUL-TIES

CONFESSION
Gal 6:17: *From henceforth let no man trouble me: for I bear in my body the marks of the Lord Jesus.*

PRAISE WORSHIP
1. Thank the Lord, for His redemptive power.
2. Prayers of confession of sins and forgiveness.
3. I release myself, from all unprofitable friendships, in Jesus' name.
4. I come against, the dark powers which have manipulated my friendship with . . . (*mention the name of the person*) and I break their powers over my life, in the name of Jesus.
5. I bind, all demonic authorities, which motivated and controlled my relationship with . . . (*mention the name of the person*) and break their authority and power over my affections, in the name of Jesus.
6. I command, all evil 'remote controllers' to loose their hold upon my affections, in the name of Jesus.
7. I release myself, from the hold of every bewitched relationship, in the name of Jesus.
8. By the blood of Jesus, I remove myself from any strange authority ever exercised over me.
9. I remove, all evil soul ties and affections, in the name of Jesus.

10. I come against, every desire and expectation of the enemy to engage me in any unprofitable relationship, in the name of Jesus.

11. I break, every ungodly relationship, in Jesus' name.

12. I break and renounce, evil soul ties, I have had or may have had with . . . . . in the name of Jesus.
    - secret societies
    - cults
    - adulterers
    - family members
    - close friends
    - organisations
    - husbands
    - past or present friends
    - acquaintances
    - wives
    - engagements
    - doctors
    - clubs
    - religious leaders
    - social organisations
    - preachers, etc.,

13. I renounce, all hidden evil soul ties, in Jesus' name.

14. I renounce, break and loose myself from all demonic subjection to any relationship, in the name of Jesus.

15. I break, all evil soul-ties and wash them away with the blood of the Lord Jesus.

16. I remove myself, from any strange authority exercised over me, in the name of Jesus.

17. I remove, all mind controlling manipulations between me and any friend or family member, in the name of Jesus.

18. I claim deliverance, from any negative affection towards anyone, in the name of Jesus.

19. Let evil affections towards me be wiped off the mind of . . . (*mention the name of the person*), in the name of Jesus.
20. Lord Jesus, I give You my affections, emotions and desires and I request that they be in submission to the Holy Spirit.
21. Praise the Lord for answered prayer.

TO ARREST UNPROFITABLE LATENESS IN MARRIAGE

CONFESSIONS
Phil. 2:9-10: Wherefore God also hath highly exalted him, and given him a name which is above every name: That at the name of Jesus every knee should bow, of things in heaven, and things in earth, and things under the earth;
Col. 2:13: And you, being dead in your sins and the uncircumcision of your flesh, hath he quickened together with him, having forgiven you all trespasses;
Rev. 12:11: And they overcame him by the blood of the Lamb, and by the word of their testimony; and they loved not their lives unto the death.
Luke 1:37: For with God nothing shall be impossible.

PRAISE WORSHIP
1. Thank the Lord because your miracle has come.
2. Ask the Lord to forgive you any sin that would hinder answers to your prayers.

Prayer Strategies for Singles

3. Lord, make known to me, the secrets of my inner life, in the name of Jesus.

4. Help me Lord, to discover my real self, in Jesus' name

5. Let every imagination, of the enemy, against my marital life be rendered impotent, in Jesus' name.

6. I refuse, to co-operate with any anti-marriage spells and curses, in the name of Jesus.

7. I cancel, every bewitchment, fashioned against my settling down in marriage, in the name of Jesus.

8. Let every force, magnetising the wrong people to me be paralysed, in the name of Jesus.

9. I break, every covenant of marital failure and late marriage, in the name of Jesus.

10. I cancel, every spiritual wedding, conducted consciously or unconsciously on my behalf, in the name of Jesus.

11. I remove, the hand of household wickedness from my marital life, in the name of Jesus.

12. Let every incantation, incisions, hex and other spiritually harmful activities working against me, be completely neutralized, in the name of Jesus.

13. I command all the forces of evil, manipulating, delaying or hindering my marriage to be completely paralysed, in the name of Jesus.

14. Let all evil anti-marriage marks, be removed, in Jesus' name.

15. Lord, restore me, to the perfect way in which You created me if I have been altered, in Jesus' name.

Prayer Strategies for Singles

16. Father, let Your fire, destroy every satanic weapon, fashioned against my marriage, in Jesus' name.
17. Lord, expose, all the schemes and plans of satan, ever devised against me, through any source and at any time, in the name of Jesus.
18. I forsake, any personal sin that has given ground to the enemy, in the name of Jesus.
19. I reclaim, all the ground I have lost to the enemy, in the name of Jesus.
20. I apply, the power in the name and blood of Jesus to my marital situation, in the name of Jesus.
21. I apply, the blood of Jesus to remove all the consequences of evil operations and oppression, in the name of Jesus.
22. I break, the binding effect, of anything of evil, ever put upon me from any source, in Jesus' name.
23. Let all the enemies of Jesus Christ, operating against my life be exposed, in the name of Jesus.
24. I sever myself, from any satanic linkage and any strange power, in the name of Jesus.
25. I remove, the right of the enemy, to afflict my plan to get married, in the name of Jesus.
26. I break, every bondage of inherited marital confusion, in the name of Jesus.
27. I bind and plunder, the goods of every strongman attached to my marriage, in the name of Jesus.

28. Let the angels of the living God, roll away the stone blocking my marital breakthrough, in Jesus' name.
29. I remove my name, from the book of seers of goodness without manifestation, in Jesus' name.
30. Let God arise, and let all the enemies of my marital breakthrough be scattered, in the name of Jesus.
31. Let the fire of God, melt away the stones hindering my marital blessings, in the mighty name of Jesus.
32. Let the cloud, blocking the sunlight of my glory and breakthrough, be dispersed, in the name of Jesus.
33. Let all evil spirits, masquerading to trouble my marital life, be bound, in the name of Jesus.
34. The pregnancy of good things within me, will not be aborted by any contrary power, in Jesus' name.
35. Lord, let wonderful changes, begin to be my lot from this week, in the name of Jesus.
36. I reject, every spirit of the tail in all areas of my life, in the name of Jesus.
37. I receive, my right match, in the name of Jesus.
38. I stand against, every spirit of discouragement, fear, worry and frustration, in the name of Jesus.
39. Lord, turn away all that would jilt, disappoint or fail me, in the name of Jesus.
40. Thank God for the victory.

TO KNOW GOD'S WILL IN MARRIAGE

Bachelors and spinsters can use these prayer points to determine the following:

(i)   whether a particular person, is God's choice for them in marriage or not
(ii) to discover secret things beneficial or detrimental to such a relationship
(iii) to implant God's wisdom into the foundation of the relationship.

Confessions: Dan. 2:2; Eph. 1:17; Psalm 25:14; Deut. 29:29

PRAISE WORSHIP

1. Thank God for the revelational power of the Holy Spirit.
2. O God, to whom no secret is hidden, make known unto me whether . . . (*mention the name of the person*) is Your choice for me in marriage, in the name of Jesus.
3. O Lord, remove from me, any persistent buried grudges, half-acknowledged enmity against anyone and every other thing that can block my spiritual vision, in the name of Jesus.
4. Let every marriage related idol, present consciously or unconsciously in my heart, be melted away by the fire of the Holy Spirit, in the name of Jesus.
5. O Lord, give unto me the Spirit of revelation and wisdom, in the knowledge of You, in Jesus' name.
6. O Lord, remove spiritual cataract from my eyes, in the name of Jesus.

7. O Lord, forgive me for every false motive or thought that has ever been formed in my heart, since the day I was born till today, in the name of Jesus.
8. O Lord, forgive me for any lie that I have ever told against any person, system or organisation, in the name of Jesus.
9. O Lord, open up my spiritual understanding, in the name of Jesus.
10. O Lord, teach me deep and secret things, in the name of Jesus.
11. O Lord, reveal to me every secret behind the marriage proposal whether beneficial or not, in the name of Jesus.
12. I refuse to fall, under the manipulation of the spirits of confusion, in the name of Jesus.
13. O Lord, teach me to know that which is worth knowing and love that which is worth loving and to dislike whatsoever is not pleasing to Your eyes, in the name of Jesus.
14. I refuse, to make foundational mistakes in marriage, in the name of Jesus.
15. Father Lord, guide and direct me in finding the partner You have ordained for me, in Jesus' name
16. I stand against, all satanic attachments that may seek to confuse my choice, in the name of Jesus.
17. If . . . (*mention the name of the person*) is not for me, God, re-direct his/her steps, in the name of Jesus.
18. I bind the activities of . . . (*pick from the list below*) in my life, in the name of Jesus.

(i) lust   (ii) ungodly infatuation

(iii) ungodly family pressure

(iv) demonic manipulation in dreams and visions

(v) attachment from/to the wrong choice

(vi) confusing revelations

(vii) spiritual blindness and deafness

19. Lord, make Your way plain before my face, in the name of Jesus.

20. O God, You who reveal secret things, make known unto me Your choice for me in marriage, in the name of Jesus.

21. Holy Spirit, open my eyes and help me to make the right choice, in the name of Jesus.

I RECEIVE IT

PRAISE WORSHIP

1. Thank the Lord because this year is your year of dumbfounding miracles, in the name of Jesus.

2. Confess these scriptures out loud: Philippians 2:9; Colossians 2:13; Rev. 12:12; Luke 1:37.

3. Lord, make known to me the secrets needed for my marital breakthrough, in the name of Jesus.

4. Help me Lord, to discover my real self, in Jesus name

5. Let every imagination of the enemy against my marital life be rendered impotent, in Jesus' name.

6. I refuse, to co-operate with any anti-marriage spells and curses, in the name of Jesus.

7. I cancel, every bewitchment fashioned against my settling down in marriage, in the name of Jesus.

8. Let every force, magnetizing the wrong people to me be paralysed, in the name of Jesus.

9. I break, every covenant of marital failure and late marriage, in the name of Jesus.　⚬

10. I cancel, every spiritual wedding, conducted consciously or unconsciously on my behalf, in the name of Jesus.

11. I remove, the hand of household wickedness from my marital life, in the name of Jesus.

12. Let every incantation, incisions, hex and other spiritually harmful activities working against my marriage, be completely neutralized, in Jesus'name.

13. I command all the forces, of evil manipulating, delaying or hindering of my marriage to be completely paralysed, in the name of Jesus.

14. Let all evil anti-marriage covenants be broken, in the name of Jesus.

15. Lord, restore me to the perfect way in which You created me if I have been altered, in Jesus' name.

16. Father, let Your fire, destroy every satanic weapon fashioned against my marriage, in Jesus' name.

17. I forsake, any personal sin that has given ground to the enemy, in the name of Jesus.

18. I reclaim, all the ground I have lost to the enemy, in the name of Jesus.

Prayer Strategies for Singles

19. Let the blood of Jesus, speak against every power working against my marriage, in the name of Jesus.
20. I apply the blood of Jesus, to remove all the consequences of evil operations and oppression, in Jesus' name.
21. I break, the binding effect, of anything of evil, ever put upon me from any source, in Jesus' name.
22. I remove, the right of the enemy to afflict my plan to get married, in the name of Jesus.
23. I break, every bondage of inherited marital confusion, in the name of Jesus.
24. I bind and plunder, the goods of every strongman's plans attached to my marriage, in Jesus' name.
25. Let the Angels of the living God, roll away, the stone blocking my marital breakthroughs, in Jesus' name.
26. Let God arise, and let all the enemies of my marital breakthrough be scattered, in the name of Jesus.
27. Let the Fire of God, melt away, the stones hindering my marital blessings, in the mighty name of Jesus.
28. Let the cloud, blocking the sunlight of my marital breakthrough be dispersed, in Jesus' name.
29. Let all evil spirits, masquerading to trouble my marital life, be bound, in the name of Jesus.
30. Lord, let wonderful changes, be my lot this year, in the name of Jesus.
31. Lord, turn away, all that would jilt, disappoint or fail me, in the name of Jesus.
32. Thank God for the victory.

BOOK ORDER

Is there any book written by Dr. D. K. Olukoya (General Overseer MFM Ministries) that you would like to have? Have you seen his latest books? To place order for this end-time materials,

State your request as follows:

Book Title(s) : . . . .

Delivery Address : . . . .

Call 0816 122 9775

God bless you.

Battle Cry Christian Ministries

... equipping the saints of God

ABOUT BCCM, MFM MINISTRIES AND THE AUTHOR Dr. D. K. Olukoya is the General Overseer of the Battle Cry Christian Ministries and Mountain of Fire and Miracles Ministries. The Mountain of Fire and Miracles Ministries' Headquarters in Lagos, Nigeria, is the largest single Christian congregation in Africa with attendance of over 120,000 in single meetings.

MFM is a full Ministry devoted to the revival of Apostolic signs, Holy Ghost fireworks, miracles and the unlimited demonstration of the power of God to deliver to the uttermost. Absolute holiness, within and without as the greatest spiritual insecticide and pre-requisite for heaven, is openly taught. MFM is a do-it-yourself Ministry, where your hands are trained to wage war and your fingers to do battle.

Dr. Olukoya holds a first class honours degree in Microbiology from the University of Lagos, Nigeria and a Ph.D. in Molecular Genetics from the University of Reading, United Kingdom. As a researcher, he has over seventy scientific publications to his credit.

Anointed by God, Dr. D. K. Olukoya is a prophet, evangelist, teacher and preacher of the Word. His life and that of his wife, Shade and their son, Elijah Toluwani are living proofs that all power belongs to God.

The Battle Cry Christian Ministries is devoted to :

(i) teaching and disseminating information on Christian spiritual warfare,

(ii) making available life-changing Christian articles and books at affordable prices and

(iii) preparing an army of aggressive prayer warriors and intercessors in this end-time.

Published by:

The Battle Cry Christian Ministries

P. O. Box 12272, Ikeja, Lagos, Nigeria. Tel/Fax (01) 4939797

ISBN 978-2947-65-2

Made in the USA
Columbia, SC
12 May 2021

37737276R00061